table talk

table talk

food
family
love

A COOKBOOK

by Carol McManus

with Brenda L. Horrigan

VINEYARD
STORIES

TABLE TALK
Text Copyright ©2008 Carol McManus

Published by
Vineyard Stories
RR1 Box 65-B9
Edgartown, MA 02539
www.vineyardstories.com

Library of Congress Control Number: 2008921655

ISBN 9780977138470

Photo credits:

Lifestyle photographs -- including the main cover image, the photo on the previous page, and the photo on this page -- are owned by Betsy Corsiglia, ©2008 Betsy Corsiglia. All rights reserved.

Food photographs are owned by Kathryn Osgood, ©2008 Kathryn Osgood. All rights reserved.

Cover design by Kolodny Dorr Media Design, Vineyard Haven, MA.
Book design by Shock Design & Associates, Inc., Atlanta, GA.

Thanks to Jane Chandler of the Beach House, Vineyard Haven, for her assistance.

Manufactured in China

*To my mother,
Dorothy Moisson*

Contents

*First we eat, then
we do everything else.*

— M.F.K. FISHER

Foreword

It's time to bring back the family meal. You might think it odd for a café owner to make such a statement. After all, my livelihood depends on people choosing to eat out. But before I owned the Espresso Love Café, I was a mom, and this I know: if you want a happy, healthy family, have most of your meals at home, together.

Sitting down to share a meal helps a family bond. Raising my kids, I was amazed how much I could learn by just listening to Maureen, Debby, Michael, Paula, and TJ chat with each other around the dinner table. The evening meal was a fixed event in our day, like sunrise and sunset. Even when my husband, a police officer, had evening duty, he almost always got home for dinner. He set the police radio on the table, we said grace, and then the kids vied to fill Dad's ears with stories from their day. Today, they laugh and tell their own kids about how Dad would lecture them ("In my day, one pair of sneakers was sufficient to play any sport") or about the time he turned up his nose at my pea soup (which so happens now to be one of my customers' favorites, thank you very much). It touches me to hear them reminisce. Our greatest memories of being a family were mostly set around that old pine dining room table.

Somehow, though, Americans have let this precious family time slip away. Only about 58 percent of U.S. families sit down together regularly for dinner. Family time has been forced into the backseat by homework, after-school activities, and even TV shows. Parents and children these days are too often ships passing in the night. Of course, some change in how we live is inevitable; the world's so different now from even just a decade ago. But I doubt kids have stopped yearning for love and attention, and what better way to show both than to sit with them, share good food, laugh, and tell stories?

Talking to my customers, and my now-grown kids, I get the idea that more and more people want to bring back the family dinner. Look at the bestseller list: Titles like *Dinner with Dad: How I Found My Way Back to the Family Table* are showing up all the time. Who can ignore study after study showing that children from families that have frequent family meals are far less likely to abuse drugs or alcohol, develop eating disorders, or engage in risky sexual behavior? (They're much more likely to do well in school, too.) More than one parent, though, has confided in me that they have no idea how to get their family back to the table. I tell them: If I could do it, anyone can.

The cooking side did come naturally to me, I admit. My mom and grandmother both loved to cook, and in their families the evening meal was not optional. Both women passed down that passion for kitchen creativity to me. I knew this for sure the day my dad brought home a new Sunbeam electric mixer. My mom had to go out on errands and assigned me some chores. The second she was out the door, I dropped the mop and started whipping up a chocolate cake. Boy, did I get in trouble. (But she liked the cake.) When I married and had kids, I did what I'd seen my mom do every day. There was no special talent involved, just some good guides and daily practice.

If you haven't regularly put together a dinner for your brood recently, it might seem intimidating, even overwhelming, to plan a meal, do the shopping, cook the food, and get everyone seated at the same time. Just take it step by step, though, and you'll find it's easier than you think. That's why I wrote *Table Talk*: to help show you how to make the family meal part of daily life again.

I've always been a mom with a job outside the home, so I remember how it feels some days, walking in the door after a tough day. The kids are cranky and hungry (or, worse, they've been hitting the chips and soda in the after-school hours). You're tired, and your briefcase is bulging with paperwork you didn't get to between nine and five. Piling everyone in the car to hit the drive-through, or calling up for takeout, might seem easier. But it's much more costly, and in more ways than one. With just a bit of planning and practice, and a guide like *Table Talk*, you'll be able to walk in the door and whip up a satisfying meal everyone will clamor for. Really!

Most of the pages in this book focus on food—getting a simple, delicious meal on the table. There's also some advice, though, on how to make these meals something your family looks forward to and gets a lot out of. (Step one: Turn off everyone's cell phone.) Scattered throughout are ideas for involving everyone in meal prep or for coping during really busy weeks. (Hint: Stay flexible. It's okay to let a basketball game or piano recital delay the start of your evening meal, as long as it doesn't regularly *preempt* it.)

You might be surprised at all the benefits you reap when you start eating at home together on a regular basis. It's easier on the wallet than eating out, of course. It's healthier, too, because you pick the ingredients and can keep an eye on things like salt, fat, and sugar. (Growing up, there was maybe one chubby child in my class. Today, according to the American Academy of Family Physicians, 15 percent of American children between the ages of six and nineteen are overweight. Fifty-nine million Americans are overweight or obese.) My guess is, though, that you'll find

Food + Family

that the most important reward of dining together is the satisfaction you'll feel from teaching the next generation what it means to be a family. That's what *Table Talk* is all about: how to create those simple daily family events that turn into tradition.

♥

About seventeen years ago, when my marriage ended, I still had five kids to raise. By that time we were living on Martha's Vineyard year-round, and I had to invent a new career to keep the roof over our heads. One night I was watching the TV show 20/20; there was a piece about the coffee boom and the rise of Starbucks. All at once, I realized that there was no place in the off-season for the Vineyard locals to get a good cup of coffee or a light lunch. I loved to cook. I love coffee. I needed a job. The solution was obvious. With the help of my kids—a small loan from one, lots of hours in the kitchen from the others—I opened the Espresso Love Café in 1991. In its first incarnation, Espresso Love was tiny, tucked away in a small corner of a hotel. Today, it's a large garden café that attracts Islanders, seasonal visitors, and even the occasional First Family.

In *Table Talk* you'll find eighty of my best-loved recipes, ones I raised my kids on and many that have graced the Espresso Love menu board for years. Every dish has been tested hundreds of times by kids and customers. I've aimed to include something for every taste and every sort of day: super-simple suppers, slightly fancier weekend and "company's coming" fare, desserts to share (and make together), even yummy make-ahead breakfasts to get everyone's day started off right.

In the sidebars, you'll find a collection of timesaving tips, serving and menu suggestions, and pointers on selecting ingredients or cooking utensils. These recipes are simple enough for even a beginning cook and use ingredients found in most supermarkets. A good family meal doesn't need fancy techniques or equipment, just a bit of your time, and love. (Okay, an oven and a stove help, too.)

There are so many things that cut into family time, but with just a bit of effort, you can keep the family meal alive in your home. *Table Talk* suggests that creating a family meal each day is not just possible, it's healthy and fun. Gathering together, sharing a meal along with the joys and frustrations of your day, is an act that binds families together. Food + Family = Love. It's an equation that's been part of my family's life for years, and it will work for you.

Espresso LOVE
edgartown
martha's vineyard

Carol McManus

EDGARTOWN, MASSACHUSETTS
APRIL 2008

See us at www.tabletalkcookbook.com

A Word About the Photographs

The authors, photographers, and publishers of this book have summered, and lived, on the island of Martha's Vineyard, Massachusetts.

And while the subject of the book—that the family dinner table should be an important part of life—is universal, we have elected to illustrate it not just with photographs of the good food from Carol McManus's kitchen, but also with pictures of the good life around us.

The Vineyard, seven miles off the Massachusetts coast, exerts a strong pull on families—those who, year-round, want to raise their family with a slightly different rhythm than is found in many mainland communities; and those who come to visit on a summer vacation and leave with wonderful memories of time spent together.

So we have included photographs of Vineyard moments: the Farmers Market, the seashore, the dog in the pickup, a youngster in a cranberry bog. And, yes, an autumn morning in the garden of Espresso Love Café.

To state our mission plainly: The book is a call to action for renewed family time and mealtime. And it comes to you, with love, from Martha's Vineyard.

—The Editors

CHAPTER ONE

The Dinner Table

The family is the
country of the heart.

— Giuseppe Mazzini

Stovetop Cheese & Pasta Supper

I DARE YOU! *This is the ultimate easy meal, and a great way to sneak in the broccoli. A recipe in Nigel Slater's* Appetite—*in my opinion, a book that should be put back into print—inspired this dish. I've simplified his recipe even more, and I dare you to find an easier, or more delicious, supper dish than this.*

PREPARATION TIME: 25 MINUTES ♥ COOKING TIME: 15 MINUTES ♥ MAKES 6 SERVINGS

INGREDIENTS

1 LB. PASTA OF YOUR CHOICE (ANYTHING WORKS WELL: PENNE, ELBOWS, SPIRAL AND TWIST SHAPES)

1 LARGE HEAD BROCCOLI (APPROXIMATELY 1 CUP FLORETS)

3 CUPS GORGONZOLA CHEESE (OR CHOOSE ANY CHEESE YOU LIKE THAT MELTS FAIRLY EASILY), BROKEN INTO PIECES

1/2 TSP. SALT

1. Prepare pasta according to package instructions.

2. Bring a small pot of water to boil, adding 1/2 tsp. salt.

3. Trim the florets off the broccoli head, then cut the uppermost, tender parts of the stalks into long thin pieces, approximately 1–2 inches long, and 1/4 inch thick. Put broccoli florets in the smaller pot of water and simmer to tenderness, approximately 3 minutes. (Taste a piece to make sure it's cooked the way you like it.) Drain the water from the pot.

4. Warm a large serving bowl (if it'll fit, put it in the oven for a couple minutes—or run it under hot water, then quickly dry). Put the cheese into it. It will start to ooze. Add the hot broccoli, and then the drained pasta.

5. Toss the cheese, broccoli, and pasta. Spoon into shallow bowls and serve.

JUMP-STARTING THE WEEK
Mondays—how do we survive them? Things got easier in my house when I made Monday night "pasta night." One less decision for me—and because pasta is my family's favorite, it helped bring everyone to the table and started our week of family dinners off right.

A MATTER OF CHOICE
Let the kids pick what pasta shape you'll use—twists, shells, bowties, whatever makes them smile. You can even mix several types together (just pick pastas with comparable cooking times).

Mac & Cheese with Prosciutto

The key to this dish is using flavorful cheese, such as the combination of Gouda, Gruyere, and Parmesan here. Prosciutto is thinly-sliced Italian ham; you can substitute a salty ham from the deli, too.

PREPARATION TIME: 25 MINUTES ♥ COOKING TIME: 30 MINUTES ♥ MAKES 8 SERVINGS

INGREDIENTS

2 CUPS ELBOW MACARONI

2 CUPS 2 PERCENT MILK

2 CUPS HALF AND HALF

2 CUPS GRATED GRUYERE CHEESE

2 CUPS GRATED GOUDA CHEESE

2 CUPS SHREDDED PARMESAN CHEESE

1/2 CUP PROSCIUTTO, OR ANY SALTY HAM, CUT INTO SMALL PIECES (ABOUT 1/2-INCH SQUARES)

1/4 TSP. NUTMEG

SEA SALT AND BLACK PEPPER, TO TASTE

1/2 CUP BREADCRUMBS, EITHER STORE-BOUGHT OR HOMEMADE (RECIPE, PAGE 11)

1. Preheat oven to 350°. Spray a 9x13-inch glass baking dish with cooking spray, and set aside.

2. Fill a large saucepan with water and boil. Add macaroni and cook until soft, but not mushy, according to package directions.

3. In a large bowl, stir together the milk, half and half, cheeses, prosciutto, nutmeg, salt, and pepper.

4. Drain pasta and pour into prepared baking dish. Pour or spoon milk and cheese mixture over pasta. Sprinkle with breadcrumbs.

5. Bake for about 20–25 minutes until the top is slightly browned. Cool slightly before serving, so dish firms up a bit.

Note: You can grate the cheese in this recipe by hand, chopping it with a knife into small pieces or using a box grater, but that's time consuming. If you don't care to invest in a food processor, consider a hand-held rotary grater. They're less than $20 and make grating cheese a snap.

If your family isn't wild about Gouda or Gruyere, make up your own signature combo, like Cheddar and Parmesan. Any flavorful combination will work.

Two Quick Crockpot Meals →

Beef Stew

Long ingredient lists can make a recipe look complicated, but both these crockpot meals have a basic, simple logic: Sauté the first few ingredients, add the next several, and in the end let everything simmer on its own until dinnertime. Couldn't be simpler!

PREPARATION TIME: 20 MINUTES ♥ COOKING TIME: 2–4 HOURS ♥ MAKES 6 SERVINGS

INGREDIENTS

1 TBSP. OLIVE OIL, AND MORE AS NEEDED

2 GARLIC CLOVES, MINCED

2 ONIONS, CUT INTO CHUNKS

2 LBS. BEEF STEW, CUT INTO CHUNKS

1 CUP RED WINE

2 SMALL CANS BEEF STOCK

1/4 CUP TOMATO PASTE

1 CUP WHOLE CANNED TOMATOES, WITH JUICE

8 NEW MEDIUM-SIZED POTATOES, QUARTERED

4 CARROTS, PEELED AND SLICED

1 TSP. SALT

FRESHLY GROUND PEPPER

1/2 TSP. DRIED BASIL

1/2 TSP. OREGANO

2 TSP. DRIED THYME, OR 1 TBSP. FRESH THYME

2 CUPS FROZEN PEAS

1. Heat oil in a large pot. Sauté garlic and onion for two minutes. Add beef, turning to brown on all sides.

2. Add wine, beef stock, and tomato paste and cook for 10 minutes.

3. Add tomatoes, potatoes, carrots, salt, pepper, basil, oregano, and thyme. Cook for 5 more minutes.

4. Transfer to a crockpot. Cook for 2 hours on high or 4 hours on low. Add peas 40 minutes before the stew is done.

5. Serve with green salad and fresh bread.

Chicken Thighs with Veggies

If you don't want to use a crockpot, cook for an hour in a 9 x 13 pan in a 350° oven.

PREPARATION TIME: 20 MINUTES ♥ COOKING TIME: 2 HOURS ♥ MAKES 6 SERVINGS

INGREDIENTS

2 TBSP. OLIVE OIL

1 MEDIUM ONION, DICED

2 GARLIC CLOVES, MINCED

1 CUP BUTTON MUSHROOMS, SLICED

SALT AND FRESHLY GROUND PEPPER

6 BONELESS CHICKEN THIGHS

1/2 CUP WHITE WINE

1 CUP CHICKEN STOCK

2 CUPS CANNED WHOLE TOMATOES, CRUSHED BY HAND

1 MEDIUM ZUCCHINI, SLICED

1 MEDIUM SUMMER SQUASH, SLICED

PINCH CAYENNE PEPPER

1 TSP. DRIED THYME LEAVES

1 TBSP. FRESH BASIL LEAVES, CHOPPED

1/2 CUP GRATED PARMESAN CHEESE

1. Heat olive oil in a large frying pan. Add onion, garlic, and mushrooms, and sauté on medium heat for 3 minutes. Salt and pepper the mixture.

2. Add the chicken thighs and cook on each side until they are lightly browned. Pour wine, chicken stock, and canned tomatoes over chicken, and cook for 5 minutes. Add the sliced zucchini and squash, cayenne pepper, thyme, and more salt and pepper. Cook for 2 minutes.

3. Place chicken mixture into a crockpot and cook for 2 hours on low. When almost finished, add basil leaves and Parmesan cheese.

A MINI RECIPE

English Muffin Pizzas

A simple meal or snack we forget. Load a platter with a few favorite toppings and gather the crew for a pizza-making buffet.

INGREDIENTS

1 PACKAGE THOMAS' ENGLISH MUFFINS

OLIVE OIL

HOMEMADE ZINGY RED SAUCE (RECIPE, PAGE 8) OR SLICES OF TOMATOES

DRIED OREGANO

FRESH GROUND PEPPER

2 CUPS, SLICED OR SHREDDED MOZZARELLA

Possible toppings: Cooked bacon, sausage, pepperoni, or vegetables such as mushrooms, small-cut pepper varieties, onions, etc.

1. Preheat broiler.
2. Lightly toast English muffins. Place on a cookie sheet. Brush top of muffins with olive oil. Put about 1 Tbsp. sauce on top, add spices, then a slice of cheese. Add desired toppings. Place muffins under broiler for about 5 minutes until cheese is melted.

Honey-Mustard Beef Stir-fry

This stir-fry tastes best served on a bed of rice. Consider brown rice, which isn't any more difficult to make, but has more fiber. Make the rice ahead, then cook the meat and veggies. You don't want too many pots to watch at the same time!

PREPARATION TIME: 20 MINUTES ♥ COOKING TIME: 20 MINUTES ♥ MAKES 4 SERVINGS

INGREDIENTS

2 TSP. VEGETABLE OIL

1 LARGE CLOVE GARLIC, CRUSHED (OR 1 TSP. PREPARED GARLIC, EITHER CRUSHED OR MINCED)

2 ONIONS, CUT INTO WEDGES

1^1/2 LBS. RUMP STEAK OR TOP OF THE ROUND STEAK, CUT INTO THIN STRIPS (HINT: FREEZE THE MEAT FOR ABOUT 1 HOUR, TO MAKE IT EASIER TO CUT THINLY)

^{1}/3 CUP DIJON MUSTARD

^{1}/4 CUP HONEY

^{1}/2 LB. FRESH OR FROZEN GREEN VEGETABLES (GREEN BEANS, SNOW PEAS, ASPARAGUS ARE ALL GOOD)

SALT AND PEPPER TO TASTE

1. Put a frying pan (use one that's at least 2 inches deep) over high heat. Add oil, garlic, and onion. Cook for 2 minutes.

2. Add the beef strips and cook about 4 minutes, stirring continuously. The meat is done when it's well-browned and no more juices are oozing from it. Add mustard, honey, and vegetables. Toss so that the meat and vegetables are all coated with the spices, honey, and oil. Cook for 2–3 more minutes, or until the vegetables are crisp-tender (which is about halfway between raw and thoroughly cooked and soft).

3. Put about a half-cup of cooked rice on each plate, then spoon the meat and vegetables on top. The mustard and honey should add enough flavor, but feel free to add a bit of salt and pepper.

Baked Italian Chicken

This simple, tasty chicken goes great with Red Bliss Potatoes (see mini-recipe) or a green salad. You can buy a small wedge of Parmesan cheese in the deli aisle, and cut off the slices with a sharp knife.

PREPARATION TIME: 20 MINUTES ♥ COOKING TIME: 45 MINUTES ♥ MAKES 6 SERVINGS

INGREDIENTS

6 ROMA TOMATOES, HALVED

3 TBSP. OLIVE OIL

SEA SALT, PLUS BLACK PEPPER, TO TASTE

3 TBSP. STORE-BOUGHT PESTO

6 BONELESS CHICKEN BREAST HALVES

8 SLICES PARMESAN CHEESE (CUT FROM A SMALL WEDGE).

12 SLICES PROSCIUTTO

1. Heat the oven to 350°. Line a baking dish with foil or parchment paper, and coat with cooking spray.

2. Place tomatoes, cut side up, in the baking dish. Drizzle with olive oil and sprinkle lightly with salt and pepper. Bake for 20 minutes.

3. Spread the pesto over the chicken breasts and top each breast with a slice of Parmesan cheese, then wrap the chicken and cheese with a slice of prosciutto (or a salty ham, sliced very thin).

4. Place the chicken in the baking dish with the tomatoes, and bake 20–25 minutes, until the chicken is cooked through.

A MINI RECIPE

Red Bliss Potatoes

A good accompaniment to Baked Italian Chicken or Quick Codfish (page 10). Red Bliss are small, red, thin-skinned potatoes, available in most supermarkets. (You can substitute white potatoes or Yukon Golds, but choose small ones, which stay much more tender than large potatoes, like Idahos.)

PREP TIME: 10 MINUTES
COOKING TIME: 50 MINUTES
MAKES 6 SERVINGS

INGREDIENTS

10 WASHED RED BLISS POTATOES

1/4 CUP OLIVE OIL

1 GARLIC CLOVE, SLICED (OR 1 TSP. PREPARED CHOPPED GARLIC)

SEA SALT AND CRACKED BLACK PEPPER

1. Preheat oven to 375°.
2. Put the potatoes in a baking dish and pour oil over them. Scatter garlic slices around the pan. Salt and pepper the potatoes.
3. Roast for about 1 hour, or until the potatoes are soft when you insert a fork.

Zingy Red Sauce

A true kitchen staple. It freezes beautifully and goes with all sorts of dishes, from meatballs to Chicken Parmesan to pizza (the English muffin or regular variety).

PREP TIME: 15 MINUTES
COOKING TIME: 45–60 MINUTES
MAKES 6 SERVINGS

INGREDIENTS

3 TBSP. OLIVE OIL

1 MEDIUM WHITE ONION CHOPPED INTO SMALL PIECES

4 CLOVES GARLIC, MASHED

2 CANS CRUSHED TOMATOES

1 TBSP. DRIED BASIL

2 TSP. DRIED OREGANO

1 TSP. SEA SALT

1/4 TSP. GROUND BLACK PEPPER

1/4 CUP RED WINE *OR* 2 TBSP. SUGAR

1. Warm olive oil in a large pan over medium heat. Sauté onions until translucent, stirring continuously for about 5 minutes.
2. Add garlic and cook 2–3 minutes, stirring continuously to avoid burning the garlic.
3. Add the crushed tomatoes, basil, oregano, salt, pepper, and wine or sugar, stirring to combine ingredients. Cover and lower heat, simmering for about an hour. Stir every 5–10 minutes to prevent sticking.

Tried & True Meatballs

A great make-lots, freeze-some recipe. Serve one night with pasta, save a batch for a meatball sub later in the week.

PREPARATION TIME: 20 MINUTES ♥ COOKING TIME: 20 MINUTES ♥ MAKES 6 SERVINGS

INGREDIENTS

1 LB. GROUND BEEF

4 CLOVES GARLIC, MASHED (OR 1 TBSP. PREPARED CRUSHED OR MINCED GARLIC)

2 TBSP. OLIVE OIL (THOUGH YOU MIGHT NEED MORE TO KEEP MEATBALLS FROM STICKING WHILE COOKING)

1 EGG

1/2 CUP ITALIAN BREADCRUMBS

1/2 CUP GRATED PARMESAN CHEESE

2 TBSP. DRIED PARSLEY FLAKES

1 TSP. OREGANO

1 BATCH ZINGY RED SAUCE (SEE MINI-RECIPE)

1. Place all ingredients (except Zingy Red Sauce) in a large bowl and mix together with your hands. Form the combined ingredients into 2-inch balls.

2. Using a large frying pan, heat the olive oil until hot, over a medium flame.

3. Brown meatballs on all sides, about 5 minutes. Don't crowd the meatballs; do them in batches if your pan is too small to accommodate them all. Remove and drain on a paper towel.

4. Finish cooking the meatballs by simmering in a pot of red sauce for 20–25 minutes. Serve meatballs on a sub or other roll or over pasta.

Everything you see I owe to spaghetti.

— SOPHIA LOREN

A MINI RECIPE

Sautéed Spinach

A great side dish to serve with any kind of meat or fish. It's also 10 minutes from start to serving plate.

PREP TIME: 5 MINUTES
COOKING TIME: 5 MINUTES
MAKES 4 SERVINGS

INGREDIENTS

2 TSP. OLIVE OIL

1 CLOVE GARLIC, MINCED (ABOUT 1/2 TSP.)

1 1/2 LBS. BABY SPINACH LEAVES

SALT AND FRESHLY GROUND PEPPER TO TASTE

♥ Heat olive oil in hot pan, then add garlic and lightly brown. Immediately add spinach and cook briefly until the leaves are wilted. Season with salt and pepper.

Quick Codfish

A trip to the fish market to pick out the filet is a fun pre-meal outing. Before frying up the fish, you can also help your children cut their piece into a fun shape with a large cookie cutter.

PREPARATION TIME: 10 MINUTES ♥ COOKING TIME: 13 MINUTES ♥ MAKES 4 SERVINGS

INGREDIENTS

2 TBSP. OLIVE OIL

2 TBSP. BUTTER

1 1/2 LBS. CODFISH (YOU MAY SUBSTITUTE HADDOCK)

SEA SALT

GROUND BLACK PEPPER

1 LEMON, CUT INTO WEDGES

1. Preheat the oven to 350°.

2. Pour enough olive oil in a heavy frying pan to cover the bottom. Heat over medium heat, then add butter and let it melt and foam. Place the fish in the oil and butter, skin side down. Cook until the bottom is lightly browned. Using a spatula, carefully turn the fish over. Sprinkle with salt and pepper.

3. Remove the fish from the frying pan and place in an oven-proof dish. Bake in oven for 8 minutes, or until it is cooked through (it's done when the fish is opaque and flakes when you touch it with a fork).

4. Cut the fish into whatever serving size you prefer (palm-sized is good). Garnish with a lemon wedge or two.

Zingy Chicken Parmesan

Here's a classic Italian American dish that my mama made and my kids (and customers) still adore. It's an entrée on its own, or—served with your favorite condiments or some Zingy Red Sauce on a hearty roll—it's a fabulous chicken sandwich.

PREPARATION TIME: 20 MINUTES ♥ COOKING TIME: 25 MINUTES ♥ MAKES 6 SERVINGS

INGREDIENTS

6 PIECES BONELESS CHICKEN BREASTS OR CHICKEN BREAST TENDERLOINS

1 EGG, LIGHTLY BEATEN

2 CUPS ITALIAN BREAD CRUMBS (SEE MINI-RECIPE)

1/2 CUP OLIVE OIL

1 CUP ZINGY RED SAUCE (RECIPE, PAGE 8)

1/4 CUP SHREDDED MOZZARELLA CHEESE

1/2 CUP QUALITY SHAVED OR SHREDDED PARMESAN CHEESE

SALT AND PEPPER TO TASTE

1. Heat the oven to 350°.

2. Rinse chicken and pat dry with a paper towel. If your pieces are on the thick side, put them in a heavy-duty plastic bag and pound with a meat tenderizer or small hammer until the chicken is an even 1/2-inch thick. One by one, drop each into the egg and then into the breadcrumbs. Shake off the excess.

3. Put enough olive oil into a large skillet to cover the bottom of the pan. Heat over medium heat until hot but not smoking. Place breaded chicken breasts in the pan and brown on the first side, about 2 minutes, then turn and brown the other side. Don't crowd the breasts; if necessary, cook them in batches.

4. Drain the breasts on a paper towel.

5. Place the chicken in a baking dish and cover with red sauce and sprinkle with mozzarella and Parmesan. Bake for 20 minutes and serve with a side order of pasta or a salad.

♥ A MINI RECIPE

Homemade Breadcrumbs

These tasty breadcrumbs are easy to make and add tons of flavor to all kinds of recipes, including my Chicken Parmesan and my Tried and True Meatballs. (I use the Italian variation, below, for those two recipes). Let the French bread sit out unwrapped the night before, so it dries out. Or cut fresh bread into slices and dry it in a 200° oven for about 10 minutes, and cool.

INGREDIENTS

1 HALF-LOAF OF FRENCH BREAD

1/2 CUP EXTRA VIRGIN OLIVE OIL

SEA SALT AND GROUND BLACK PEPPER

1. Heat oven to 400°.
2. If you're using a food processor, pulse pieces of bread into small pieces; otherwise you can crumble it by hand.
3. Put bread into bowl and toss with olive oil until lightly moistened. Sprinkle with sea salt and pepper.
4. Spread on a cookie sheet and bake until slightly brown, approximately 10 minutes. Let cool, then keep in an airtight container.

Variation: For Italian Breadcrumbs, add 1 tsp. dried oregano and 1 tsp. dried basil, along with salt and pepper.

Thyme-Touched Roast Chicken with Rosemary, Potatoes, and Carrots

PREPARATION TIME: 10 MINUTES ♥ COOKING TIME: 1 1/2 HOURS ♥ MAKES 4 SERVINGS

INGREDIENTS

ONE 3- TO 4-LB. CHICKEN, RINSED, WITH GIBLETS REMOVED

KOSHER OR SEA SALT

BLACK PEPPER

1 BUNCH FRESH THYME (AT LEAST 10 SPRIGS)

1 BUNCH FRESH ROSEMARY (AT LEAST 10 SPRIGS)

2 CLOVES GARLIC, PEELED

KITCHEN STRING (ABOUT 1 FOOT LONG)

2 TBSP. BUTTER, MELTED

4 MEDIUM POTATOES (ANY TYPE WILL WORK, BUT YUKON GOLD ARE ESPECIALLY GOOD)

6 MEDIUM CARROTS

2 TBSP. OLIVE OIL

1. Preheat oven to 350°.

2. Season chicken cavity lightly with salt and pepper. Stuff chicken cavity with half of the thyme, rosemary, and garlic. Tie the legs together with kitchen string and place in a roasting pan. Drizzle melted butter over chicken.

3. Cut the potatoes into halves. Cut the carrots into halves and quarters. (I like to peel my potatoes, but it's not necessary. I recommend peeling the carrots, though.)

4. Put the potatoes in a bowl and toss with the olive oil. Then add remaining rosemary and thyme. Lightly salt and pepper the potatoes and place them into the roasting pan around the chicken. Add the carrots.

5. Roast the chicken and veggies for about 1 1/2 hours.

ANOTHER ONE-POT WONDER. *Younger kids might get a kick out of stuffing the bird with herbs, drizzling it with butter, or placing the veggies in the pan around the bird.*

The onion is the truffle of the poor.

— ROBERT J. COURTINE

Roasted Butternut Squash

Load up at the local farm stand and make a double batch, then use the extra to make Butternut Squash and Apple Soup (recipe, page 40).

PREP TIME: 5 MINUTES
COOKING TIME: 25 MINUTES
MAKES 4 SERVINGS

INGREDIENTS

2 LBS. BUTTERNUT SQUASH, PEELED AND CUT INTO CHUNKS

3 TBSP. OLIVE OIL

1 TSP. FRESH THYME

SALT AND PEPPER TO TASTE

1. Preheat oven to 400°.
2. Combine all ingredients in a large bowl. Spread out on a cookie sheet and bake for 25 minutes, or until squash is soft when you pick it with a fork.

Vegetable Ragoût

Think Local!
A trip to the closest farm stand is a fun, low-cost family outing. Go in July or August for fresh squash, tomatoes, and basil for this high-flavor dish.

PREPARATION TIME: 20 MINUTES ♥ COOKING TIME: 20 MINUTES ♥ MAKES 4 SERVINGS

INGREDIENTS

2 TBSP. OLIVE OIL	SALT AND FRESHLY GROUND PEPPER
1 TBSP. BUTTER	1 TBSP. FRESH BASIL, CHOPPED
1 TSP. MINCED GARLIC	1 TSP. FRESH OREGANO, CHOPPED
1 LARGE SHALLOT, MINCED	1 TSP. FRESH THYME, CHOPPED
1 ZUCCHINI, WASHED AND SLICED	1/2 CUP RED WINE
1 SUMMER SQUASH, WASHED AND SLICED	1 TSP. TOMATO PASTE
3/4 LB. WILD MUSHROOMS (CHANTERELLES)	1 CUP TOMATO, COARSELY CHOPPED

1. In a large sauce pan, heat oil and butter. Add garlic and shallots and cook about 1 minute. Add zucchini, squash, and mushrooms, and cook until soft, about 8 minutes. Season with salt and pepper. Add the basil, oregano, and thyme.

2. Add wine and cook for about 2 minutes, then add tomato paste and cook for another minute, mixing thoroughly. Add the tomato and cook for 5 minutes.

CHAPTER TWO

The Breakfast Table

As a child my
family's menu
consisted of two choices:
take it or leave it.

— BUDDY HACKETT

Carol's Crunch Time Granola with Dried Fruits and Almonds

Easy to make ahead and store, and it will wean the kids off sugary, additive-laden store-bought cereals. A quick breakfast that will stick to their ribs.

PREPARATION TIME: 25 MINUTES ♥ COOKING TIME: 20 MINUTES ♥ MAKES 6 SERVINGS

INGREDIENTS

1/2 CUP DRIED CRANBERRIES

1/2 CUP DRIED CHERRIES

3/4 CUP RAISINS

1 1/2 CUPS SLICED APRICOTS, CUT INTO SMALL PIECES

6 CUPS OATS

1 1/2 CUPS COCONUT

1 1/2 CUPS SLICED ALMONDS

3/4 CUP CANOLA OIL

3/4 CUP HONEY

1. Preheat oven to 355°. Cover a large cookie sheet well with pan spray.

2. Cut up the dried fruit, and set aside.

3. In a large bowl, combine oats, coconut, almonds, oil, and honey together, mixing thoroughly. Spread evenly on the prepared pan. Place in the oven for about 20 minutes, turning frequently, so it cooks evenly. When the granola is a nice golden color all over, take it out of the oven and let it cool.

4. Put all ingredients in a large bowl and combine, then store in an airtight container to preserve freshness.

This recipe can be doubled.

A family in harmony will prosper in everything.

— CHINESE PROVERB

Pancakes with Fruit

Commercial pancake mix is expensive and filled with additives—two negatives that make the convenience of "mix and cook" hardly worth the effort. Instead, take a few extra minutes to mix up your own pancakes.

PREPARATION TIME: 10 MINUTES ♥ COOKING TIME: 5 MINUTES ♥ MAKES 4 SERVINGS

INGREDIENTS

1 EGG

1 CUP BUTTERMILK OR 2 PERCENT MILK

1/2 TSP. VANILLA EXTRACT

1 CUP FLOUR

3 TBSP. SUGAR

1 TBSP. BAKING POWDER

1/8 TSP. NUTMEG

1/2 TSP. SALT

2 TBSP. CANOLA OIL PLUS EXTRA FOR PAN

1/2 CUP BLUEBERRIES OR THINLY SLICED BANANAS

1. In a small bowl, whisk together egg, milk, and vanilla. In a second larger bowl, mix flour, sugar, baking powder, nutmeg, and salt. Add wet ingredients to dry ones, whisking until the lumps disappear. Whisk in the oil.

2. Heat a little oil in a large skillet. Drop batter by spoonfuls into the pan. When the top of the pancake begins to bubble, drop fruit on top and flip the pancake. Cook for another minute. Serve with maple syrup, butter and sugar, jam, or yogurt.

A TOPPING ALTERNATIVE

Maple syrup is yummy, but can get boring, too. Jazz it up by heating it with a handful of fresh or frozen berries. Simmer until the skins of the berries burst, flavoring (and tinting) the syrup.

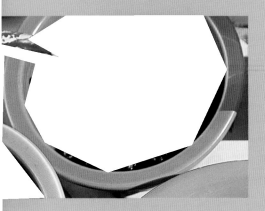

Veggie Omelet with Feta

PREPARATION TIME: 15 MINUTES ♥ COOKING TIME: 10 MINUTES ♥ MAKES 2 SERVINGS

INGREDIENTS

3 EGGS

$1/4$ TSP. SALT

FRESHLY GROUND PEPPER TO TASTE

PINCH CAYENNE

$1/8$ TSP. DRIED BASIL

4 TSP. BUTTER

$1/4$ CUP CRUMBLED FETA CHEESE

2 TBSP. CHOPPED YELLOW ONION

1 TBSP. CHOPPED RED BELL PEPPER

1 TBSP. CHOPPED YELLOW BELL PEPPER

1. Whisk eggs in a bowl with salt, pepper, cayenne, and basil until frothy.

2. In an 8-inch nonstick skillet, melt the butter over medium-high heat. Add the eggs and cook until just set on the bottom. Sprinkle cheese, onions, and red and yellow peppers across the omelet. Using a heat-resistant spatula, go around the edges to loosen eggs.

3. When eggs are almost set, flip omelet to the other side. Cook for 1 more minute. Slide onto a plate and fold in half.

Food is an important part of a balanced diet.

— FRAN LEIBOWITZ

Love's Frittata

PREPARATION TIME: 15 MINUTES ♥ COOKING TIME: 10 MINUTES ♥ MAKES 4 SERVINGS

INGREDIENTS

1 TBSP. BUTTER

1 TBSP. VEGETABLE OIL

2 BIG POTATOES, SLICED

1 MEDIUM ONION, CHOPPED

1/4 POUND MUSHROOMS, SLICED

1 RED BELL PEPPER, CHOPPED

SALT AND BLACK PEPPER TO TASTE

1/2 TSP. OREGANO OR MARJORAM

1/2 TSP. CRUSHED, DRIED RED PEPPER

6 LARGE EGGS

1/4 CUP MILK

2 SLICED TOMATOES

12 PITTED BLACK OLIVES

2 SCALLIONS, DICED

1/4 LB. CHEDDAR OR SWISS CHEESE, GRATED

BIG HELPING OF PARMESAN CHEESE

1. Preheat the oven to 325°.

2. Butter and oil go into a nonstick frying pan over moderate heat. Toss in the sliced potatoes and cook about 10 minutes; they should be crispy. Shake the pan every few minutes so the potatoes don't stick.

3. Add onions, mushrooms, and red pepper. When the onion begins to go clear, season with salt, pepper, oregano (or marjoram), and the crushed, dried red pepper.

4. In a bowl, beat the eggs with the milk and pour on top of the ingredients in the pan. Shut off the heat. Decorate with sliced tomatoes, olives, and scallions on top of the eggs; top with grated cheese and Parmesan. Place into the oven for 15–20 minutes, just until set (the middle should be firm when you shake the pan).

5. Let it sit for a few minutes, then cut the frittata into wedges and serve. Hot, warm, or cold, it makes a wonderful wake-up meal.

All happiness depends on a leisurely breakfast.

— JOHN GUNTHER

Blueberry Muffins

Muffins are a breakfast staple. But we've all eaten those tough, cakey kind that taste more like sawdust than a morning delicacy. The key to any muffin is to barely mix the ingredients so they stick together, making them moist and delicate.

PREPARATION TIME: 15 MINUTES ♥ COOKING TIME: 35–45 MINUTES ♥ MAKES 12 LARGE MUFFINS

INGREDIENTS

1 CUP BUTTER, SOFTENED	4 TSP. BAKING POWDER
2 CUPS SUGAR	4 CUPS ALL-PURPOSE FLOUR
4 EGGS	1 CUP MILK
2 TSP. VANILLA	2 1/2 CUPS BLUEBERRIES
1 TSP. CINNAMON	EXTRA SUGAR FOR MUFFIN TOPS

1. Preheat oven to 375°. Line muffin pan with baking cups.

2. Using an electric mixer, beat softened butter until creamy. Add sugar and beat until light and fluffy. Add eggs, one at a time, and beat thoroughly. Stir in vanilla, cinnamon, and baking powder. Mix at medium-high speed for one minute.

3. Add half the flour, and mix at the lowest speed (or stir in flour and milk by hand) until barely combined. Pour in 1/2 cup milk and stir until just combined. Mix in the remaining flour and milk, being careful not to overmix the batter. Stir in blueberries.

4. Scoop the batter into the prepared muffin pan. Sprinkle the tops with sugar. Bake until muffins are browned on top and spring back when lightly pressed, approximately 35–45 minutes. Let cool in pan before removing.

Variation: For Triberry Muffins, use 1 cup blueberries, 1/2 cup strawberries, and 1/2 cup raspberries. Prepare as directed.

Apple Strudel Muffins

PREPARATION TIME: 15 MINUTES ♥ COOKING TIME: 35–45 MINUTES ♥ MAKES 12 LARGE MUFFINS

INGREDIENTS

3 CUPS FLOUR

1 CUP SUGAR

4 TSP. BAKING POWDER

1/2 TSP. BAKING SODA

2 TSP. CINNAMON

1/4 TSP. ALLSPICE

4 EGGS

2 CUPS SOUR CREAM (LOW-FAT IS FINE)

1/2 CUP BUTTER, MELTED

2 GRANNY SMITH APPLES, PEELED AND CHOPPED

TOPPING INGREDIENTS

2 TBSP. BUTTER, SOFTENED

4 TBSP. ALL-PURPOSE FLOUR

3 TBSP. SUGAR

1/4 TSP. CINNAMON

1/2 CUP CHOPPED WALNUTS

1. Preheat oven to 375°. Line 12-cup muffin pan with baking cups.

2. Prepare topping: Put ingredients in a small bowl and, using your fingers, mix together until lumpy. Set aside.

3. In a large bowl, stir together flour, sugar, baking powder, baking soda, cinnamon, and allspice.

4. In a separate bowl, whisk eggs, sour cream, and melted butter until smooth. Stir in chopped apples.

5. Pour wet ingredients into the dry. Mix until just moistened and combine. Be careful not to overmix.

6. Fill muffin pans and sprinkle with topping. Bake for about 30 minutes, or until muffin springs back when lightly pressed.

FOR VARIETY . . .

A muffin is mainly flour, sugar, butter, baking powder, egg, and cinnamon. The other ingredients you can mix and match. Try it with my basic blueberry muffin, by making one of these little changes:

- Replace the sugar with vanilla sugar (recipe below).
- Replace the blueberries with the same amount of another fruit (raspberries or diced strawberries, peaches, apple).
- Add 1 Tbsp. of grated lemon or orange zest.
- Add 1/2 tsp. of a favorite spice (nutmeg, ginger, allspice).
- Add a cup of chopped nuts.

A MINI RECIPE

Vanilla Sugar

In an airtight container, place 1 fresh vanilla bean, split lengthwise, and cover with 1 cup of sugar. Let sit for at least two days (it will keep indefinitely).

Presidential Muffins
(Patriotic—but Non-Partisan)

PREPARATION TIME: 15 MINUTES ♥ COOKING TIME: 30–35 MINUTES ♥ MAKES 10 LARGE MUFFINS

INGREDIENTS

3 CUPS ALL-PURPOSE FLOUR

3/4 CUP SUGAR

1 TBSP. BAKING POWDER

1/2 CUP BUTTER, MELTED

8 OZ. CREAM CHEESE, SOFTENED

1 CUP MILK

1 TSP. VANILLA

2 EGGS

3/4 CUP BLUEBERRIES

1/2 CUP STRAWBERRIES, CHOPPED

EXTRA SUGAR FOR TOP OF MUFFINS

1. Preheat oven to 375°. Grease muffin tins or use paper baking cups.

2. In a large bowl, sift together flour, sugar, and baking powder. Set aside.

3. In a food processor, combine melted butter, cream cheese, milk, vanilla, and eggs. Process until smooth. Pour liquid into dry ingredients and stir just until combined. Fold in fruit.

4. Scoop batter into muffin cups. Lightly sprinkle tops with sugar. Bake for 30 minutes, or until muffins spring back when lightly pressed.

Variation: For Peach Raspberry Cream Cheese Muffins, substitute 3/4 cup chopped peaches and 1/2 cup raspberries for the blueberries and strawberries.

"Saved for Bill"

Before Bill Clinton came for his first vacation on the Vineyard, a New York Times reporter wandered around asking Islanders what they thought of the planned visit. I told him I was planning a special Presidential Muffin. I phoned the White House to ask what foods President Clinton liked. "He likes everything," they said.

My two basic muffins—blueberry and cream cheese—provided the blue and white. I just needed some red. I started experimenting and came up with the Presidential Muffin, loaded with blueberries, strawberries, and cream cheese. During the week the Clinton family was on-Island, I made these every day and put one on a pedestal with the sign "Saved for Bill." But he never dropped by.

The next summer, my son TJ was opening the shop early in the morning when the Secret Service arrived, followed by Bill, Hillary, and Chelsea. TJ grabbed the phone (the Secret Service tried to stop him, but he waved them off: "If I don't call Mom, she'll never forgive me!") I was there just in time to present President Clinton with the Presidential Muffin.

The next thing I knew, the Muffin was in all the papers, and even on Japanese TV. It's still a big seller. Whenever someone can't decide which muffin they want, I ask: "Do you have some big decisions to make?" If so, I recommend the Presidential.

Sunrise Sandwich

PREPARATION TIME: 15 MINUTES ♥ COOKING TIME: 10 MINUTES ♥ MAKES 4 SERVINGS

INGREDIENTS

8 STRIPS OF COOKED BACON

4 ENGLISH MUFFINS, SPLIT

4 EGGS

1/2 CUP MILK

SALT AND PEPPER TO TASTE

VEGETABLE COOKING SPRAY

4 SLICES PEPPER JACK CHEESE, OR SOME OTHER CHEESE OF YOUR CHOICE

2 TBSP. BUTTER

1. Cook bacon until crisp.

2. Toast English muffins and butter them.

3. Whisk eggs, milk, salt, and pepper. Spray a large frying pan with vegetable spray, place over medium heat and pour egg mixture into it, stirring to scramble.

4. While the eggs are cooking, melt cheese over the bacon in a microwave.

5. Put 1/4 of cooked eggs on side of buttered English muffin, top with bacon and cheese, and cover with other half of muffin.

6. Eat immediately.

Never work before breakfast; if you have to work before breakfast, eat your breakfast first.

— JOSH BILLINGS

Hazelnut Chocolate Chip Scones

PREPARATION TIME: 20 MINUTES ♥ COOKING TIME: 20–22 MINUTES ♥ MAKES 7 SCONES

INGREDIENTS

2 1/2 CUPS ALL-PURPOSE FLOUR

1/3 CUP COLD BUTTER, CUT INTO CHUNKS

1 TBSP. BAKING POWDER

2/3 CUP BROWN SUGAR

1/2 CUP GROUND HAZELNUTS (IF WHOLE, GRIND IN FOOD PROCESSOR)

1/2 CUP SEMI-SWEET CHOCOLATE CHIPS

1/4 CUP BUTTERMILK

3/4 CUP HAZELNUT COFFEE OR REGULAR COFFEE, COOLED

PARCHMENT PAPER OR COOKING SPRAY

1. Preheat oven to 400°.

2. Lightly spray a cookie sheet or line with parchment paper.

3. In a food processor bowl (or using a pastry cutter), process flour, butter, and baking powder until medium-sized granules appear.

4. Place processed ingredients in a large bowl and add sugar. Mix lightly. Stir in hazelnuts and chocolate chips. Make a well in the middle of the ingredients and add milk and coffee.

5. Lightly mix until ingredients are incorporated, being careful not to overmix.

6. Using an ice cream scooper, drop onto the prepared cookie sheet. Cook for about 20–22 minutes or until lightly browned on top and cooked in the middle.

7. These can be frozen or put into an airtight container to eat later. Reheat in the oven for about 5 minutes.

A MINI RECIPE

Banana-Berry Smoothie

A great way to get your daily serving of fruit. Be sure to buy fruit with no added sugar (like Trader Joe's brand).

PREP TIME: 3 MINUTES
MAKES 1 SERVINGS

INGREDIENTS

3 ICE CUBES

8 OZ. SKIM OR LOW-FAT MILK

1/4 CUP FROZEN SLICED BANANA

1/4 CUP FROZEN BLUEBERRIES

1/4 CUP FROZEN STRAWBERRIES

♥ Place all ingredients in a blender. Pulse until smooth. If it is too thick, add more milk.

Other fruit, fresh or frozen, can be substituted, such as raspberries, pineapple, and cherries.

Basic Blueberry Scones

The key to great scones is a gentle touch. Blend the ingredients, but don't overmix.

PREPARATION TIME: 10 MINUTES ♥ COOKING TIME: 15–20 MINUTES ♥ MAKES ABOUT 7 SCONES

INGREDIENTS

2 1/2 CUPS ALL-PURPOSE FLOUR

1/2 CUP COLD BUTTER, CUT INTO CHUNKS

1 TBSP. BAKING POWDER

2/3 CUP SUGAR

1 TSP. LEMON ZEST

1 CUP BUTTERMILK

1 TSP. VANILLA

1 CUP BLUEBERRIES

PARCHMENT PAPER OR COOKING SPRAY

1. Preheat oven to 400°.

2. Lightly grease cookie sheet or cover with parchment paper.

3. In a food processor, pulse in flour, butter, and baking powder until butter is in small granules. (If you don't have a food processor, use your fingers to mix until little chunks form. Really!) Don't over process.

4. Pour ingredients from food processor into a large mixing bowl. Add in sugar and zest. Make a well in the middle of the mix and add buttermilk and vanilla. Mix lightly until all ingredients are just combined. Stir in blueberries.

5. Use an ice cream scoop and drop onto prepared cookie sheet. Bake 15–20 minutes.

Note: If you don't have buttermilk on hand, substitute by adding a tablespoon of lemon juice or vinegar to a cup of milk.

VARIATION

To make cranberry coconut scones, substitute 1 cup frozen cranberries and 1/2 cup coconut for the blueberries, and leave out the lemon zest.

French Coffeecake

This is based on a recipe I found while on vacation, in the St. Thomas Reformed Church cookbook. It's a lovely touch for a special brunch—and travels well, in case you're off to see family or friends. I don't know what's French about it—perhaps it's the presentation. With its layers of chocolate, walnuts, and cinnamon sugar, it looks beautiful when sliced.

PREPARATION TIME: 15 MINUTES ♥ COOKING TIME: 1 HOUR

INGREDIENTS

1 CUP BUTTER, SOFTENED

1¹/2 CUPS SUGAR

1 CUP SOUR CREAM

1 TSP. VANILLA

5 EGGS

3 CUPS ALL-PURPOSE FLOUR

2 TSP. BAKING POWDER

1 TSP. BAKING SODA

TOPPING INGREDIENTS:

1 TSP. CINNAMON

$^{1}/_{2}$ CUP SUGAR

1 CUP CHOCOLATE CHIPS

1 CUP WALNUTS, CHOPPED

1. Preheat oven to 350°. Grease well a 10-inch tube or Bundt pan.

2. In a small bowl, combine ingredients for the topping and set aside.

3. In a large mixing bowl, beat butter and sugar at high speed until light and fluffy. Add the sour cream and vanilla. Beat in the eggs, one at a time, mixing thoroughly after each addition.

4. Mix the flour, baking powder, and baking soda together, then slowly add those ingredients to the butter and egg mixture. Beat for several minutes; the batter should be light and creamy.

5. Pour half the batter into prepared pan. Cover the batter with half the topping mixture. Pour in the remaining batter, then top with rest of topping mix.

6. Bake cake for 1 hour or until a cake tester inserted in the center comes out clean.

I want a little sugar in my bowl, I want a little sweetness in my soul.

— NINA SIMONE

CHAPTER THREE

The Healthy Table

*It's bizarre that the produce manager is
more important to my children's health
than the pediatrician.*

— MERYL STREEP

Fat-Free Muffin

Sometimes mistakes turn out to be lucky. One day I forgot to add oil to my muffin batter. But the result wasn't half bad. I tried another batch, adding applesauce to provide moisture, and created a new standard for Espresso Love's bakery case.

PREPARATION TIME: 15 MINUTES ♥ COOKING TIME: 35 MINUTES ♥ MAKES 12 MUFFINS

INGREDIENTS

3 EGG WHITES OR 2 WHOLE EGGS

1 1/2 CUPS BROWN SUGAR

1 1/2 CUPS PUREED BANANA (OR 3 MASHED BANANAS)

3/4 CUP APPLESAUCE

2 TSP. VANILLA

2 TSP. CINNAMON

1 TSP. NUTMEG

1 TSP. ALLSPICE

1 1/2 CUPS ALL-PURPOSE FLOUR

1 1/2 CUPS WHOLE-WHEAT FLOUR

1 CUP OATS

1 TBSP. BAKING POWDER

2 TSP. BAKING SODA

2 1/2 CUPS FROZEN OR FRESH BLUEBERRIES, STRAWBERRIES, RASPBERRIES, OR MIXTURE

1. Preheat oven to 375°. Prepare a muffin tin with paper baking cups, or grease the tins.

2. In a large bowl, whisk together the egg whites or eggs with the brown sugar. Add bananas, applesauce, and vanilla. Whisk until smooth.

3. In a separate bowl, mix together cinnamon, nutmeg, allspice, flour, whole-wheat flour, oats, baking powder, and baking soda. Stir the dry ingredients into the wet until just combined. Gently stir in the fruit.

4. Fill prepared muffin pan and bake 30 minutes, or until the muffins are evenly browned and spring back when pressed.

Childhood is a short season.

— HELEN HAYES

Tomato Pumpkin Bisque

This soup takes only about 20 minutes to make, but it is delicious.

PREPARATION TIME: 5 MINUTES ♥   COOKING TIME: 15 MINUTES ♥   MAKES ABOUT 6 SERVINGS

INGREDIENTS

2 TBSP. CANOLA OIL

1 LARGE ONION, CHOPPED

3 CANS KITCHEN-READY TOMATOES

2 CUPS CHICKEN STOCK

1 CUP PUMPKIN PUREE (CANNED IS FINE, BUT DON'T USE PUMPKIN PIE FILLING)

1/2 CUP REAL MAPLE SYRUP

SALT AND FRESHLY GROUND PEPPER TO TASTE

1. Heat oil in a large pot. Sauté onion until soft and transparent. Add tomatoes and chicken stock. Then add pumpkin puree, maple syrup, and salt and pepper.

2. Cook for about 15 minutes, until soup is hot. Keep tasting the soup, and add more salt and pepper if needed.

IF YOUR KIDS BALK AT CHUNKY SOUPS, *just pour the soup into a blender, blend, and then reheat on the stove.*

♥

Worries go down better with soup.

— JEWISH PROVERB

Spinach Tortellini Soup

PREPARATION TIME: 20 MINUTES ♥ COOKING TIME: 20 MINUTES ♥ MAKES ABOUT 6 SERVINGS

INGREDIENTS

1 CUP TRICOLOR TORTELLINI (MEAT OR CHEESE), COOKED PER PACKAGE INSTRUCTIONS

2 TBSP. OLIVE OIL

1 SMALL ONION, CHOPPED

1 TBSP. CHOPPED GARLIC

1 1/2 CUPS CHOPPED MUSHROOMS

2 CUPS CANNED ITALIAN WHOLE TOMATOES, WITH LIQUID AND CHOPPED INTO CHUNKS

1/2 CUP WHITE WINE

10 CUPS HOMEMADE OR GOOD CANNED CHICKEN STOCK (USE COLLEGE INN OR OTHER PREMIUM CANNED STOCK)

1 8-OZ. BOX FROZEN CHOPPED SPINACH, DEFROSTED AND DRAINED

2 TBSP. FRESH BASIL OR 1 1/2 TSP. DRIED BASIL

1 1/2 TSP. OREGANO

SALT AND PEPPER TO TASTE

1/2 CUP GRATED PARMESAN CHEESE

1. Cook tortellini, drain, and set aside.

2. In a large, deep pan, heat oil over medium heat and lightly brown chopped onion and garlic. Add mushrooms and cook until soft. Add chopped tomatoes and cook for about 5 minutes. Add the wine to deglaze. Stir in chicken stock. Add defrosted spinach, basil, oregano, and salt and pepper to taste. Cook over medium heat for about 10 minutes, until stock is hot. Add cooked tortellini and reheat.

3. Serve in bowls and sprinkle with grated cheese.

Table Talk Conversation Starters

BIRTHDAY WISHES
Who has a birthday coming up? Dinnertime is the perfect time to let the birthday boy or girl let everyone know what a perfect day would look like!

Butternut Squash and Apple Soup

Use either fresh squash or leftover Roasted Butternut Squash (recipe, page 14).

PREPARATION TIME: 20 MINUTES ♥ COOKING TIME: 50 MINUTES ♥ MAKES ABOUT 6 SERVINGS

INGREDIENTS

2 SLICES BACON

3 TBSP. CANOLA OIL

3 LEEKS, CHOPPED FINE AND WASHED WELL

2 TBSP. MINCED GARLIC

1/2 BAY LEAF

SALT AND PEPPER TO TASTE

3 LBS. BUTTERNUT SQUASH, PEELED AND CUT UP INTO CHUNKS

3 GRANNY SMITH APPLES, PEELED AND CHOPPED

6 CUPS CHICKEN STOCK

4 OZ. SOUR CREAM

1 TSP. NUTMEG

4 TBSP. SOUR CREAM

1. In a skillet, cook bacon until crisp and drain, reserving fat. Crumble bacon.

2. In a heavy saucepan, heat canola oil and bacon fat (no more than 1 1/2 Tbsp.); cook leeks, garlic, and bay leaf with salt and pepper to taste over moderate heat, stirring until softened.

3. Add squash, peeled and chopped apple, chicken stock. Simmer mixture, covered, until squash is very tender, about 40 minutes. Discard bay leaf.

4. In a blender puree mixture in batches, transferring as pureed to a clean saucepan, using chicken stock to thin soup if it is too thick.

5. Whisk in sour cream, add nutmeg, salt or pepper to taste, and heat soup over moderately low heat until hot (do not boil).

6. Serve soup topped with crumbled bacon.

Chicken and Rice Soup

PREPARATION TIME: 20 MINUTES ♥ COOKING TIME: 1¹/2 HOURS ♥ MAKES ABOUT 6 SERVINGS

INGREDIENTS

2 TBSP. CANOLA OIL

1 LARGE ONION, FINELY CHOPPED

2 LARGE GARLIC CLOVES, MINCED

2 CELERY STALKS, CHOPPED

10 CUPS CHICKEN STOCK

1 MEDIUM PARSNIP, PEELED, TRIMMED AND CUT INTO SMALL CHUNKS

1 MEDIUM TURNIP, PEELED, TRIMMED, AND CUT INTO SMALL CHUNKS

3 MEDIUM CARROTS, PEELED AND THINLY SLICED

2 BAY LEAVES

1 TSP. DRIED THYME LEAVES

3/4 TSP. DRIED TARRAGON LEAVES

1/4 TSP. GROUND CELERY SEED

1/2 TSP. FRESHLY GROUND PEPPER

1¹/2 TO 2 LBS. BONE-IN CHICKEN BREASTS, SKINS REMOVED

1/2 CUP UNCOOKED LONG-GRAIN WHITE RICE

SALT TO TASTE

1. In a large soup pot, heat the oil, then add the onion, garlic, and celery. Sauté for 3 minutes or until onion is soft. Add all the remaining ingredients except chicken and rice.

2. Bring soup to a boil. Cover, lower heat, and simmer about 20 minutes. Add the chicken and simmer an additional 40 minutes or until chicken is tender.

3. Remove the soup from heat. With a large shallow spoon, skim fat from top and discard. Remove chicken breasts and set aside. Remove bay leaves and discard.

4. Return soup to heat. Add rice and bring to a boil. Cover, lower heat, and simmer 20–25 minutes or until rice is tender.

5. Meanwhile, remove the chicken from the bone and cut into small pieces. When rice is tender, return chicken meat to pot. Add salt to taste.

Not-Your-Everyday Veggie Burger ("The Mama")

My daughter Maureen named this recipe after I had a fabulous veggie burger on vacation and went nuts trying to replicate it after I got home. The secret is the garbanzo beans, instead of the bulgur most recipes recommend. These can be either fried or baked.

PREPARATION TIME: 20 MINUTES ♥ COOKING TIME: 20 MINUTES ♥ MAKES 8–10 BURGERS

INGREDIENTS

1 TBSP. OLIVE OIL (IF USING FRYING PAN)

2 SCALLIONS, CHOPPED

1 TSP. GARLIC, CHOPPED

1/2 WHOLE VIDALIA OR OTHER SWEET ONION

3 CUPS DRAINED GARBANZO BEANS

1/4 CUP TAHINI

3 EGGS

1 CARROT, CHOPPED

1/4 CUP PARMESAN CHEESE

1/4 CUP FETA CHEESE

1/2 TSP. SALT

PEPPER TO TASTE

FRESH ROSEMARY AND CILANTRO TO TASTE

1 1/2 CUPS BREAD CRUMBS

1. Preheat oven to 350°, or prepare a frying pan with a small amount of vegetable oil.

2. Put all ingredients except bread crumbs into a food processor. Pulse until well combined. Put ingredients into a large bowl, add bread crumbs, and mix well. Form into patties.

3. If baking, place on cookie sheet and bake for 20 minutes. If frying, cook until lightly browned on each side and warm in the middle.

Note: These can be put in a freezer or refrigerator for later use. They will keep in the freezer for two months, and in the refrigerator for one week.

Here's to Bonnie

For fourteen years Bonnie Corbeil was proprietor of Luscious Licks, one of my favorite places to grab a bite on the island of St. John. But she wouldn't hand out her recipes, so I had to invent my own version. I didn't mind. Everything about Bonnie's place inspired me—the spiritual quotes on her walls, her healthy and innovative menu, and particularly the way she cared for the community. (After Hurricane Marilyn in 1995, Bonnie created a low-cost "local's platter" to feed her neighbors.) Maybe this dish should really be called The Bonnie Veggie Burger.

Grilled Veggie Salad

Kids often turn up their noses at cold crunchy bowls of salad, but put veggies on a grill and they turn sweet and soft. You can even give the larger spinach leaves a quick toss over the flames.

PREPARATION TIME: 15 MINUTES ♥ MAKES 4 SERVINGS

INGREDIENTS

4 CUPS BABY SPINACH, WASHED

2 CUPS GRILLED EGGPLANT, PORTABELLA MUSHROOMS, RED AND YELLOW BELL PEPPERS, ZUCCHINI, OR A MIX OF ANY OF THESE VEGETABLES

1 TBSP. PINE NUTS

GENEROUS CHUNK OF BLUE CHEESE, CRUMBLED

FRESH BASIL DRESSING (RECIPE BELOW)

1. Grill the vegetables until they're soft.

2. Put spinach in a large salad bowl and top with vegetables, pine nuts, and cheese. Mix lightly. Drizzle dressing over all, and toss thoroughly.

Fresh Basil Dressing

INGREDIENTS

1/4 CUP RICE WINE VINEGAR

1/4 CUP FRESH BASIL LEAVES, CHOPPED

3/4 TSP. SUGAR

1/2 TSP. SALT

1/4 TSP. FRESHLY GROUND PEPPER

1/2 CUP EXTRA VIRGIN OLIVE OIL

♥ Combine vinegar, basil, sugar, salt, and pepper into bowl of food processor. Slowly add olive oil while the blender is running. Blend until smooth.

Table Talk
Conversation Starters

NEWS YOU CAN USE

When you're skimming the paper, see if there's topic that might spark a conversation. If it's the day of the Westminster Kennel Club Dog Show, for instance, start a debate at the dinner table about what's the best breed of dog, and why.

Love Salad

When I travel, I hunt—for new tastes, new recipes. I found this salad in a small deli when I was visiting my daughter, Debby, in San Francisco. Double up on the Raspberry Vinaigrette ingredients; the dressing will keep for weeks in your fridge.

PREPARATION TIME: 20 MINUTES ♥ MAKES 4 SERVINGS

INGREDIENTS

1 HEAD ROMAINE LETTUCE, WASHED AND CHOPPED

2 GRANNY SMITH APPLES, SLICED AND CORED

1/2 CUP GOAT CHEESE, CRUMBLED

1/4 CUP WALNUT HALVES

RASPBERRY VINAIGRETTE (RECIPE BELOW)

1. Put lettuce into a large salad bowl. Arrange apples, goat cheese, and walnut halves on top.

2. Sprinkle with Raspberry Vinaigrette. Toss lightly, and serve immediately.

Raspberry Vinaigrette

INGREDIENTS

3/4 CUP THAWED FROZEN UNSWEETENED RASPBERRIES

1/4 CUP RASPBERRY VINEGAR

1 CLOVE GARLIC, PEELED

2 TBSP. HONEY

1/2 TSP. SALT

1 CUP MILD VEGETABLE OIL (CANOLA OR SAFFLOWER)

♥ Place all ingredients except oil in bowl of a food processor. Process until blended. Slowly pour the oil through the top of the blender, pulsing until emulsified.

Note: This can be used on other salads as well. Double up the ingredients and store for the next week.

To make a good salad is to be a brilliant diplomatist— the problem is entirely the same in both cases. To know exactly how much oil one must put with one's vinegar.

— OSCAR WILDE

Horseradish Mayonnaise

INGREDIENTS

1 CUP MAYONNAISE

1 TSP. HORSERADISH; TRY GOLD'S FRESHLY GRATED AT THE SUPERMARKET

1 TSP. LEMON JUICE

♥ Mix all ingredients together and use as a spread on shrimp wraps. Also great on roast beef sandwiches.

Spicy Shrimp Wrap

PREPARATION TIME: 10 MINUTES ♥ COOKING TIME: 5 MINUTES ♥ MAKES 4 LARGE SERVINGS

INGREDIENTS

2 TBSP. OLIVE OIL

$1/2$ TSP. MINCED GARLIC

2 CUPS LARGE FRESH OR FROZEN SALAD SHRIMP (IF FROZEN, DEFROST ACCORDING TO PACKAGE DIRECTIONS)

2 TSP. CAYENNE PEPPER

1 TBSP. RED PEPPER FLAKES

SALT AND PEPPER TO TASTE

HORSERADISH MAYONNAISE (SEE MINI-RECIPE)

4 LARGE WHEAT WRAPS

2 CUPS MESCLUN (GREENS)

2 TOMATOES, CHOPPED

2 TBSP. CHOPPED RED ONION

1. Heat oil in a large pan. Add garlic and sauté for 1 minute. Add the shrimp and sprinkle with combined cayenne pepper and red pepper flakes. Sprinkle with a little salt and pepper. Cook for about 3 minutes; make sure shrimp is coated with spices, and is done but not overcooked. Remove pan from heat.

2. Spread about 1 tsp. Horseradish Mayonnaise over prepared wraps. Layer greens, tomatoes, and onions onto the wraps. Top with cooked shrimp. Roll, and cut in half.

Grilled Chicken Wrap with Guacamole

An excellent addition to any picnic basket.

PREPARATION TIME: 10 MINUTES PLUS MARINATING TIME ♥ COOKING TIME: 20 MINUTES
MAKES 2 SERVINGS

INGREDIENTS

2 CHICKEN BREASTS, BONELESS

SALT AND PEPPER TO TASTE

1 CUP PAUL NEWMAN'S ITALIAN SALAD DRESSING FOR MARINATING

4 LARGE WRAPS, ANY KIND

¹/4 CUP GUACAMOLE (SEE MINI-RECIPE)

2 CUPS MESCLUN (GREENS)

1 TOMATO, SLICED THINLY

4 TBSP. CHOPPED RED ONION

4 SLICES HAVARTI DILL CHEESE

1. Split chicken breasts in half. Place in dish and sprinkle with salt and pepper. Pour salad dressing over chicken, cover, and refrigerate in marinade for as little as an hour or up to overnight.

2. Prepare outdoor grill or preheat oven broiler. Grill or broil chicken about 5 minutes on each side, or until poultry is no longer pink in the middle. Slice chicken into 4 or 5 pieces.

3. To assemble chicken wrap, coat wraps with 1 Tbsp. guacamole. Layer greens, tomato, onion, and cut-up chicken breast, then Havarti cheese. Roll and cut in half. Serve with more Guacamole, if you wish.

A MINI RECIPE

Guacamole

PREP TIME: 10 MINUTES

INGREDIENTS

2 FIRM BUT RIPE AVOCADOS

2 TBSP. FRESH CILANTRO, CHOPPED

1 SMALL RED JALAPEÑO PEPPER, MINCED (DO NOT USE SEEDS)

1 TBSP. LEMON JUICE

1. Peel avocados and place in a bowl. Mash with fork. Add cilantro, jalapeño pepper, and lemon juice. Combine all ingredients and continue to mash until all lumps are gone.

2. Serve with the chicken wrap or as a dip.

Lobster Quesadillas

My friend Beth and I went to Mexico for a vacation a few years ago. There was a great restaurant connected to the hotel where we stayed. On the menu was lobster quesadillas. I think we had them every day for lunch while we were there.

MAKES 4 QUESADILLAS

INGREDIENTS

2 TBSP. CANOLA OIL

8 FLOUR TORTILLAS, THE 6-INCH KIND

1 ½ LBS LOBSTER MEAT, FRESH OR FROZEN, COARSELY CHOPPED

2 CUPS GRATED MONTEREY JACK CHEESE

SALT AND PEPPER TO TASTE

1. Heat oil in a large skillet. Place a tortilla in the pan, top with lobster meat. Salt and pepper, then put about ½ cup cheese on lobster. Top with another tortilla. Cook on one side for 2 minutes, then flip over and cook second side for another 2 minutes, making sure the cheese has melted. Remove from pan and cut into quarters.

2. Serve the quesadillas with guacamole (recipe, page 47), salsa, and sour cream.

Katama Bay Scallops

On the Vineyard, everyone waits in anticipation for bay scallops to come into season. When they do, you'll see men, women, and children in waders out in the ponds, searching the sandy bottom for the shellfish. What's your most highly prized local food?

PREPARATION TIME: 15 MINUTES ♥ COOKING TIME: 10 MINUTES ♥ MAKES 2 SERVINGS

INGREDIENTS

1 LB. LINGUINE

2 TSP. OLIVE OIL

1 CUP THINLY SLICED RED PEPPER

1 CUP THINLY SLICED RED ONION

1 CLOVE GARLIC, MINCED

¾ LB. BAY SCALLOPS

½ CUP WHITE OR ROSÉ WINE

3 TBSP. DIJON MUSTARD

¼ CUP CHOPPED PARSLEY

1. Bring a large pot of salted water to boil. Add linguine and cook according to pasta directions.

2. While linguine is cooking, heat olive oil in a medium sauté pan over medium-high heat. Add red pepper, onion, and garlic. Sauté, stirring often, until the vegetables are soft, about 3 minutes.

3. Add the scallops and cook for 30 seconds. Add the wine and simmer for 1 or 2 minutes, to reduce the liquid in the pan and concentrate the flavor. Stir in mustard and parsley and heat through, being careful not to overcook the scallops.

4. Serve over drained linguine.

Variation: Along with the mustard and parsley, add to the scallops 1½ tsp. fresh thyme leaves, 1 medium ripe tomato seeded and chopped.

Garlic Mashed Potatoes

There's nothing complicated about mashed potatoes, and you can make them extra special with just a bit of garlic. Use ground white pepper, if you want to keep the end result a light, creamy color.

COOKING TIME: 25 MINUTES

INGREDIENTS

4 LARGE RUSSET POTATOES, PEELED AND CUT INTO SLICES (ABOUT $1/4''$ THICK)

1 TSP. SALT

3 TBSP. HALF-AND-HALF

2 TBSP. BUTTER

2 TBSP. CRUSHED GARLIC CLOVES

SEA SALT AND WHITE PEPPER, TO TASTE

1. Place potatoes in a medium-size saucepan and add enough water to just cover. Bring to a boil, then lower flame so the potatoes are simmering. Cook for about 20–25 minutes, until the potatoes are soft when pierced with a fork.
2. Drain the water from the pan.
3. Add the butter, half-and-half, garlic, salt and pepper. Heat for just a minute while butter melts.
4. Remove the pan from the heat and using either a potato masher or electric mixer mash the potatoes to the desired consistency.

Lime-Seared Halibut over Baby Spinach

Get the pan very hot before you add the fish (and don't use a Teflon-coated pan). Sear the fish on both sides and then let the fish finish cooking in the oven. This is a little complicated, but well worth the effort.

PREPARATION TIME: 20 MINUTES ♥ COOKING TIME: 20 MINUTES ♥ MAKES 2 SERVINGS

INGREDIENTS

1 LB. FRESH HALIBUT

2 TSP. OLIVE OIL

1 TBSP. BUTTER

FOR LIME-TARRAGON MARINADE

2 TSP. EXTRA-VIRGIN OLIVE OIL

2 CLOVES GARLIC, MINCED

1 SMALL SHALLOT, MINCED

2 SPRIGS FRESH TARRAGON, MINCED, OR $1/2$ TSP. DRIED TARRAGON LEAVES

1 TSP. GRATED LIME ZEST

JUICE OF 2 LIMES

FOR CARAMELIZED WALNUTS

$1/4$ CUP WALNUT PIECES

1 TSP. SUGAR

FOR SPINACH SALAD BASE

2 TSP. OLIVE OIL

1 CLOVE GARLIC, MINCED

$1^1/2$ LBS. BABY SPINACH LEAVES

SALT AND FRESHLY GROUND PEPPER TO TASTE

1. *For marinade*, combine the olive oil, garlic, shallots, tarragon, lime zest, and half the lime juice. Marinate the halibut inside the refrigerator for 30–45 minutes.
2. *For walnuts*, prepare the walnuts by placing them in a dry nonstick pan on medium heat. Sprinkle with sugar and cook until they are shiny and brown, 4–5 minutes, shaking the pan continuously. Remove from heat and let cool.
3. Preheat oven to 375°.
4. Heat a heavy-bottomed, oven-proof pan over medium-high heat. Add 2 tsp. olive oil and 1 Tbsp. butter. Once butter has melted, add the fillets and cook until browned

on one side, 2–3 minutes. Flip the fish over, put into the oven, and roast until the fish is just cooked through, about 10 minutes.

5. Take fish out of oven and put on 2 plates, keeping warm. Deglaze the pan by adding rest of lime juice and heating, stirring to loosen any bits of fish. Pour pan juices over fish and continue to keep warm while spinach cooks.

6. *For spinach salad base*, heat 2 tsp. olive oil in hot pan, add garlic, and lightly brown. Immediately add spinach and cook briefly until leaves are just wilted. Season with salt and pepper.

7. Place spinach on the plates and reposition halibut on top of the greens. Top with caramelized walnuts.

Spread the table and contention will cease.

— ENGLISH PROVERB

Approach love and cooking
with reckless abandon.

— THE DALAI LAMA

TJ's Austin Salad

PREPARATION TIME: 20 MINUTES ♥ COOKING TIME: 10 MINUTES ♥ MAKES 4 SERVINGS

INGREDIENTS

4 CUPS BABY SPINACH

2 GRILLED CHICKEN BREAST, SPLIT IN HALF

WHOLE GRILLED PORTABELLA MUSHROOMS, ZUCCHINI, AND RED ONION, CUT INTO LARGE CHUNKS

1/2 CUP CRUMBLED FETA CHEESE

WALNUT OIL VINAIGRETTE (RECIPE BELOW)

SALT AND PEPPER

♥ Put spinach in a large salad bowl. Add sliced chicken breast, grilled veggies, and feta cheese. Mix lightly and dress with the Walnut Oil Vinaigrette.

Walnut Oil Vinaigrette

INGREDIENTS

1/2 CUP TOASTED WALNUTS

1/8 CHOPPED ONION

1/4 CUP WALNUT OIL

1/4 CUP RICE WINE VINEGAR

1/4 CUP WATER AT ROOM TEMPERATURE

1. Preheat oven to 350°.

2. Toast walnuts in oven for 10 minutes. Cool.

3. Put all ingredients in a food processor and blend until emulsified.

A MINI RECIPE

Herbed Croutons

INGREDIENTS

2 CUPS STALE FRENCH BREAD, CUT INTO CUBES

1/4 CUP OLIVE OIL

1 TSP. DRIED ROSEMARY LEAVES

1 TSP. DRIED THYME LEAVES

1 TSP. DRIED OREGANO LEAVES

1. Preheat oven to 375°.
2. Put bread cubes onto a cookie sheet. Pour olive oil over bread, using your hands or a spatula to coat well. Sprinkle herbs over bread and mix again.
3. Bake for about 15 minutes, until bread is lightly browned.
4. Use on top of soup or add to salads for a bit of crunch.

CHAPTER FOUR

The Weekend Table

The discovery of a new dish does more
for the happiness of mankind than
the discovery of a star.

— ANTHELME BRILLAT—SAVARIN

French Toast

INGREDIENTS

4 LARGE EGGS

1 1/4 CUPS MILK

3 TBSP. BROWN SUGAR

3/4 TSP. VANILLA EXTRACT

1/8 TSP. NUTMEG

1/2 TSP. CINNAMON

8 SLICES STALE CINNAMON-RAISIN BREAD

2 TBSP. BUTTER, AND MORE IF NEEDED FOR COOKING

ADDITIONAL BUTTER FOR TOPPING

MAPLE SYRUP TO TASTE

POWDERED SUGAR

1. Preheat oven to 300°

2. In a large bowl, whisk together the eggs, milk, brown sugar, vanilla, nutmeg, and cinnamon.

3. Place the bread flat into a large casserole dish and cover with the egg mixture. Let soak for 2 to 3 minutes.

4. Heat a large skillet over medium-high heat. Melt the butter in the pan. Place as many slices of soaked bread that will fit in one layer on the pan. Cook until golden brown, about four minutes per side. Remove pieces as they brown and place them on a baking sheet and keep warm in the oven. Continue cooking until all slices are browned.

5. Melt more butter as needed and cook the rest of the slices of bread.

6. Sprinkle with powdered sugar and serve with syrup.

That touch of nutmeg—fresh ground, if you have the time—makes all the difference.

Hide-the-Spinach Meatloaf

Those little iron-packed leaves keep the meat so moist. Serve with carrots and pota-toes, and your kids will get a full day's supply of veggies in one meal!

PREPARATION TIME: 20 MINUTES ♥ COOKING TIME: 1 HOUR ♥ MAKES 6 SERVINGS

INGREDIENTS

1 TBSP. OLIVE OIL

1 MEDIUM ONION, DICED

2 CLOVES GARLIC, MINCED

1 (8 OZ.) PACKAGE FROZEN CHOPPED SPINACH, DEFROSTED AND WITH WATER SQUEEZED OUT

2 LBS. GROUND CHUCK OR SIRLOIN

2 EGGS

1/2 CUP DRIED ITALIAN BREADCRUMBS

1/2 CUP GRATED PARMESAN CHEESE

1/2 TSP. SALT

FRESH GROUND PEPPER TO TASTE

1. Preheat oven to 350°.

2. In a small skillet, warm olive oil over low heat. Add onion and sauté until soft but not browned. Add garlic and sauté for 30 seconds more. Add spinach and sauté for about 5 minutes. Remove from heat.

3. In a large bowl, mix the ground beef, eggs, bread crumbs, Parmesan cheese, salt, and pepper. Add the cooked spinach, mixing thoroughly.

4. In a 9x13-inch baking pan (glass is preferred), shape the meatloaf into a rectangle. Bake for about an hour, taking care not to overcook or the meat will dry out. The meatloaf can be a little pink in the middle.

For Smaller Hands

Children love to help in the kitchen, and there are plenty of important tasks for them to do:

♥ *Mixing:* salad dressings; sandwich spread ingredients
♥ *Spreading:* sandwich spreads on bread; cookie dough in pan (for bar cookies)
♥ *Scraping:* bowls with a rubber spatula
♥ *Measuring:* spices, flour, sugar
♥ *Punching:* bread dough
♥ *Rolling:* pie and pizza crusts
♥ *Tossing:* salads

Pizza for Everyone →

Get a party going with a weekend pizza night. Younger kids will love making the yeast bubble and watching the dough rise. Older teens can make a grocery store run for the toppings. Let each person take a turn rolling out his or her dough as thin or thick as they want.

Basic Pizza Dough

I've been making this pizza dough for about thirty-five years. It can be wrapped in plastic and kept in the refrigerator for five days, or placed in the freezer for two weeks.

PREPARATION TIME: 60 MINUTES (INCLUDING TIME TO RISE) ♥ COOKING TIME: 20 MINUTES
MAKES ENOUGH FOR 2 9– OR 10– INCH PIZZAS OR 2 CALZONES

INGREDIENTS

3 TBSP. OLIVE OIL (PLUS ADDITIONAL FOR OILING BOWL)

3 CUPS ALL-PURPOSE FLOUR

1 TSP. SALT, PREFERABLY KOSHER OR SEA SALT

1 CUP WARM WATER

1 PKG. YEAST (1/4 OZ.)

1 TSP. SUGAR

1. Oil a large bowl.

2. Put 2 cups flour and salt in a food processor with a steel blade. Pulse for a few seconds.

3. Put warm water in a separate bowl, add the yeast, and sprinkle sugar on top. Mix for 20 seconds, and let stand for about 5 minutes or until it becomes creamy.

4. Add the oil 1 Tbsp. at a time to the flour mixture through the processor's top, pulsing 20 seconds between additions. Alternate yeast water and remaining 1 cup of flour, pulsing after each addition, until both are combined. Process until a ball forms.

5. Place the dough into the oiled bowl, cover with plastic wrap, and let it stand in a warm place to rise for 1 hour. Punch the dough down. Follow recipe directions (pages 59–62) to form either pizza or calzones.

Margherita Pizza

PREPARATION TIME: 15 MINUTES ♥ COOKING TIME: 20–25 MINUTES ♥ MAKES ONE 10–INCH PIZZA

INGREDIENTS

NONSTICK VEGETABLE SPRAY

PIZZA DOUGH (HALF OF BASIC PIZZA DOUGH RECIPE)

1 TBSP. EXTRA VIRGIN OLIVE OIL

1 LARGE RIPE TOMATO, SLICED THIN

SALT AND PEPPER TO TASTE

8 OZ. FRESH MOZZARELLA, SLICED

1/4 CUP FRESH BASIL LEAVES

1. Preheat oven to 400°.

2. Grease pizza pan with vegetable spray.

3. Roll out pizza dough on a floured surface to fit the pizza pan. Brush dough with olive oil.

4. Arrange the tomato slices over the pizza dough. Salt and pepper to taste. Arrange fresh mozzarella slices over the tomatoes. Place basil leaves randomly on the cheese.

5. Bake for 20–25 minutes or until dough is golden brown and the cheese is melted.

Practice Makes Perfect

Experience taught me early on that the best time to try a new dish is NOT when you're expecting company; there's pressure enough! So be sure to try out the recipes in this chapter on your family first.

California Pizza

PREPARATION TIME: 20 MINUTES ♥ COOKING TIME: 20–25 MINUTES ♥ MAKES ONE 10–INCH PIZZA

INGREDIENTS

CORNMEAL

PIZZA DOUGH (HALF OF BASIC PIZZA DOUGH RECIPE, PAGE 58)

BLACK OLIVE TAPENADE (RECIPE, PAGE 99)

1 GRILLED LONG EGGPLANT (AUBERGINE) SLICED LONGWISE, BRUSHED WITH OLIVE OIL, AND COOKED UNTIL SOFT ON OUT-DOOR GRILL OR UNDER OVEN BROILER

2 CUPS MESCLUN (GREENS)

1/2 CUP TOMATO, DICED SMALL

1/2 CUP CUCUMBER, DICED SMALL

NONSTICK SPRAY

1. Preheat oven to 425°.

2. Spray pizza pan, then sprinkle with cornmeal.

3. Roll out pizza dough on a floured surface to fit the pan.

4. Spread Black Olive Tapenade over the dough. Cut the grilled eggplant into small pieces, and place evenly on top of the Black Olive Tapenade. Cook in oven until crust is browned, about 20–25 minutes.

5. Take pizza out of the oven and cool for a few minutes. In the meantime, toss greens, tomatoes, and cucumbers in a bowl. Place salad on top of the pizza, cut into slices, and serve.

"SURPRISE ME" — *Ask the kids to make a pizza for you with whatever combination they want. We are always telling our kids to try new things, but it's more effective if we also demonstrate that sort of bravery!*

Meat and Cheese Calzone

PREPARATION TIME: 15 MINUTES ♥ COOKING TIME: 25–30 MINUTES ♥ SERVES 1 OR 2 PEOPLE

INGREDIENTS

½ Basic Pizza Dough (page 58)
(for 2 calzones, use the entire recipe)

¼ lb. boiled ham, sliced thin

¼ lb. Genoa salami, sliced thin

¼ lb. sliced mozzarella cheese

1 egg, beaten

1. Preheat oven to 400°. Lightly grease a cookie sheet.

2. On a floured surface, roll out the pizza dough into a 9x12-inch rectangle. Down the center of the dough, place 2 slices of the ham, then 3 or 4 slices of the salami on top of the ham, then 3 slices of cheese on top of the salami. Fold over one side of the dough to cover the meat and cheese. Crimp it along the edge to seal.

3. Repeat the same procedure on the folded part of the pizza dough, then fold the other side over and seal the edge carefully with your fingers.

4. Cut three slits on top; brush the whole calzone with the beaten egg.

5. Put on cookie sheet and bake for 25 minutes. The cheese should melt out of the slits.

Variation: This could also be made with sautéed vegetables and mozzarella cheese. Layer and cook the same way.

In the 1970s, when I lived in the Boston area, I was director of a child care center. We would have a yearly potluck night, and parents had to bring the recipe for the food they brought. Meat and Cheese Calzone is one of the recipes. When I would have soup for dinner, I always served this with it, to encourage my children to eat their soup. Bribery sometimes is a good thing!

Shiretown Ham

You can learn a lot chatting up the local butcher, the supermarket cheese manager, and the farm stand owner. The owner of Shiretown Meats, our wonderful Vineyard butcher, turned me on to this "dressed up" way of serving ham.

PREPARATION TIME: 20 MINUTES ♥ COOKING TIME: 1 HOUR ♥ MAKES 4–6 SERVINGS WITH SOME LEFTOVERS

INGREDIENTS

1 PKG. (2 DOZ.) COMMERCIALLY PREPARED GINGERSNAP THIN COOKIES

1 JAR STONEWALL KITCHEN'S MOLASSES BOURBON MUSTARD*

1 FULLY COOKED SPIRAL-CUT SMOKED HAM

1. Preheat oven to 350°.

2. Mash gingersnaps into crumbs. (You can do this by putting the cookies into a freezer baggie and rolling a rolling pin over them. Or use a food processor.) In a bowl, combine the cookie crumbs with the mustard to make a paste.

3. Put the ham into a heavy roasting pan. Spread the cookie-mustard paste over the entire ham.

4. Bake for 1 hour.

Tip: If you can't find this mustard, make your own version. Take a small jar of Dijon mustard you like and stir in 2 Tbsp. molasses. You can add a couple spoonfuls of bourbon, but it's not crucial.

I come from a family where gravy is considered a beverage.

— ERMA BOMBECK

Crispy Balsamic Chicken Wings

For a perfect fall Saturday afternoon, gather the crew, cheer on the team, and enjoy these sweet wings.

PREP TIME: 10 MINUTES, PLUS AT LEAST
12 HOURS MARINATING TIME
COOKING TIME 25 MINUTES
MAKES 4 SERVINGS

INGREDIENTS

2 LBS. CHICKEN WINGS

2/3 CUP BALSAMIC VINEGAR

3 LARGE SCALLIONS, THINLY SLICED

1. In a large bowl, combine chicken wings, vinegar, and scallions. Toss well to evenly coat the wings. Cover and refrigerate overnight.
2. When ready to cook, let chicken wings come to room temperature.
3. Preheat oven to 450°.
4. Place wings on a baking sheet in a single layer. Bake for about 25 minutes, until crispy and brown.

Tuna with Mint, Garlic, and Soy

My friend Michael Altman, a chef who has a lovely bed-and-breakfast in the south of France, taught me this recipe. It's great on a grill, but you can broil it in the oven, too.

PREPARATION TIME: 10 MINUTES PLUS MARINATING TIME ♥ COOKING TIME: 6 MINUTES
MAKES 2 SERVINGS

INGREDIENTS

2 TUNA STEAKS (1-INCH OR MORE THICK)

SEA SALT

OLIVE OIL

1 GARLIC CLOVE, MINCED

1 TBSP. SOY SAUCE

1 TBSP. CHOPPED MINT

1 LEMON, CUT INTO WEDGES

1. Rub tuna steaks with salt and olive oil. Let them stand for a half hour.
2. While steaks are resting, heat up the grill or turn on the oven broiler.
3. Mix together the garlic, soy, and mint. Rub the seasoning over the tuna.
4. Broil or grill the fish for 2–3 minutes per side.
5. Serve with lemon wedges.

Grilled Skirt Steak

Grilling out adds fun to any meal. Skirt steak is flavorful but so inexpensive you can invite the neighbors over without busting the budget. The key to keeping skirt steak tender is to grill it quickly. Serve leftovers the next day on a crusty roll with lettuce and tomato and a bit of Garlic Mayonnaise.

PREPARATION TIME: 1 HOUR ♥ COOKING TIME: 4 MINUTES ♥ MAKES 4 SERVINGS

INGREDIENTS

$1/2$ CUP OLIVE OIL

$1/2$ CUP LIME JUICE

$1/3$ CUP LIGHT SOY SAUCE

5 SCALLIONS, CHOPPED

2 LARGE GARLIC CLOVES

$1/2$ TSP. RED PEPPER FLAKES

$1/2$ TSP. CUMIN

$1/4$ CUP BROWN SUGAR

2 LBS. SKIRT STEAK

1. Make marinade by whisking together all ingredients but steak.

2. Cut steak into three pieces and lay in a 9x13-inch glass dish. Pour marinade over it, turning steak once or twice to coat. Cover with plastic wrap and refrigerate for at least 1 hour.

3. Prepare outdoor grill and remove steak from marinade. Cook steak over hot grill for 2 minutes on each side. When done, cut against the grain and serve with mashed potatoes and a green salad.

A MINI RECIPE

Garlic Mayonnaise

INGREDIENTS

1 CUP MAYONNAISE

1 TSP. MINCED GARLIC CLOVE

PEPPER TO TASTE

♥ Mix well. Can be kept in refrigerator for a week.

Baby-Back Ribs

PREPARATION TIME: 10 MINUTES ♥ COOKING TIME: 2 HOURS, 15 MINUTES ♥ MAKES 6 SERVINGS

INGREDIENTS

2 RACKS BABY-BACK RIBS

FAVORITE RUB FOR RIBS*

FAVORITE BARBECUE SAUCE

SALT

FRESHLY GROUND PEPPER

1. Preheat oven to 350°.

2. Cut ribs in half and put them on a cookie sheet. Season with the rub. Bake for about 2 hours or until they're falling off the bone.

3. Just before they're done, preheat your outdoor grill or start your charcoal briquettes.

4. Remove ribs from oven, sprinkle on more rub, coat with barbecue sauce and salt and pepper to taste. Cook on the hot grill for about 15 minutes.

*My meat man suggests Montreal Chicken Seasoning by McCormick.

Grilled Corn on the Cob

COOKING TIME: 10 MINUTES ♥ MAKES 6 SERVINGS

INGREDIENTS

6 EARS FRESH CORN

6 TBSP. MELTED BUTTER

SALT

♥ Prepare on outdoor or indoor grill. Remove husks and silk from corn. Brush ears with melted butter. Put on grill for about 10 minutes, turning often. There will be light grill marks. Remove and salt to taste.

Table Talk
Conversation Starters

A CENTERPIECE

Family heirlooms and old photos make a nice table centerpiece. Decorate the dinner table with some, and let their history start the conversation.

Black Bean Salad

A great make–ahead dish. The flavors combine and get better day after day, so make extra and serve it again later in the week (perhaps on a picnic).

PREPARATION TIME: 24 HOURS PLUS 15 MINUTES ♥ COOKING TIME: 2 HOURS ♥ MAKES 4 SERVINGS

INGREDIENTS

2 CUPS DRIED BLACK BEANS

2 CUPS FRESH CORN

1/2 RED PEPPER, DICED

1/4 CUP CILANTRO, TORN OR CHOPPED INTO SMALL PIECES

4 CHOPPED GREEN ONIONS

3/4 TBSP. MINCED GARLIC

1 1/2 TBSP. SHERRY VINEGAR

1 TSP. LEMON JUICE

1 TBSP. OLIVE OIL

1 TSP. HONEY

1/4 TSP. SALT

FRESHLY GROUND PEPPER TO TASTE

1/2 TSP. CUMIN

1. Soak black beans overnight. The next day, empty out the water and rinse the beans, checking to make sure there are no rocks in the beans.

2. Put them into a large pot, cover with water, and bring to a boil. Reduce heat and simmer for 2 hours or until they are soft. Drain and let cool.

3. Remove corn from cob. Mix the corn with the black beans. Add the red pepper, cilantro and green onions.

4. In a separate bowl, mix the garlic, cumin, sherry vinegar, lemon juice, olive oil, honey and salt and pepper. Add all the ingredients together and mix lightly.

Children need models rather than critics.

— JOSEPH JOUBERT

Stuffed Chicken Breasts with Roasted Red Pepper Tapenade

This dish can be served hot, at room temperature, or chilled. Keep a batch of the tapenade on hand; it's a tasty sandwich spread and also good on bread or crackers. That plus a salad makes a nice, light lunch.

PREPARATION TIME: 20 MINUTES ♥ COOKING TIME: 40 MINUTES ♥ MAKES 4 SERVINGS

INGREDIENTS

2 WHOLE CHICKEN BREASTS, BONELESS AND SKINLESS AND CUT INTO HALF

4 OZ. GOAT CHEESE, AT ROOM TEMPERATURE

1 TBSP. OLIVE OIL, FOR BRUSHING CHICKEN

1/4 CUP CHOPPED PARSLEY

FOR SPINACH STUFFING:

1 TBSP. OLIVE OIL

2 CLOVES GARLIC, MINCED

1 SHALLOT, MINCED

1 TSP. MINCED FRESH THYME LEAVES

6 CUPS BABY SPINACH LEAVES

SALT AND PEPPER TO TASTE

FOR TAPENADE:

1/2 CUP DRAINED CHOPPED JARRED ROASTED RED PEPPERS

3 TBSP. PITTED AND CHOPPED KALAMATA OLIVES

1 TBSP. CHOPPED CAPERS

1 TSP. BALSAMIC VINEGAR

1. Preheat oven to 375°.

2. Pound chicken breasts lightly to make them thinner.

3. For spinach stuffing, heat olive oil in a large skillet over medium high heat. Sauté the garlic, shallot, and thyme for 2 minutes until softened. Add the spinach and sauté for 1 minute longer, or until just wilted. Season with salt and pepper, and remove the skillet from heat. Let cool.

4. For tapenade, put red peppers, olives, capers, and balsamic vinegar into bowl of a food processor. Process until a paste forms.

5. Place about $1/4$ cup of the spinach mixture in the center of each pounded chicken breast. Evenly divide the goat cheese among the chicken breasts, placing a small piece over the spinach. Top with 1 Tbsp. red pepper tapenade.

6. Fold the top of the breast over the filling to form a package, sealing the bottom of the chicken packages wherever needed. Place the chicken on a baking pan. Cover with aluminum foil and bake for 25 minutes.

7. Uncover, brush the chicken with a little olive oil, and cook an additional 10 minutes, or until the chicken is brown.

8. Place the chicken on a serving platter and sprinkle with parsley.

Lasagna with Sausage and Mozzarella

PREPARATION TIME: 25 MINUTES ♥ COOKING TIME: 30–35 MINUTES ♥ MAKES 8 SERVINGS

This Lasagna is the ideal weekend cooking project/make-ahead dinner. Whip it up on a Saturday afternoon (no-boil noodles cut the prep time in half) and stash it in the freezer.

INGREDIENTS

1 LARGE ONION, CHOPPED

2 GARLIC CLOVES, CHOPPED

2 LBS. SWEET SAUSAGE

4 CUPS ZINGY RED SAUCE (RECIPE, PAGE 8)

1 EGG

2 CUPS PART-SKIM RICOTTA

2 TBSP. PARSLEY FLAKES

TABLE SALT AND PEPPER (TO TASTE)

1 CUP PARMESAN CHEESE, GRATED

1 PACKAGE NO-BOIL LASAGNA NOODLES

1 LB. MOZZARELLA, SHREDDED

COOKING SPRAY

1. Preheat oven to 375°.

2. Coat a large frying pan with cooking spray, and cook the chopped onion and garlic over medium heat until onions are soft and almost clear in color. (*Stir continuously, so they don't burn.*)

3. If the sausage is in a casing, cut open and crumble the meat into the pan with the onions and garlic. Cook for about 10 minutes, stirring occasionally. Add the Zingy Red Sauce, and simmer on low heat for about 15 minutes.

4. In a bowl, lightly beat the egg, then add ricotta, parsley, salt, and pepper. Add 1/2 cup of the Parmesan cheese.

5. Pour 1 cup of sauce into a 9x13-inch baking dish. Make sure the dish is at least 2–3 inches deep. Spread sauce around, to coat the bottom of the pan. Cover with one layer of lasagna noodles. Cover the noodles with more red sauce. Then drop the ricotta mixture by spoonfuls onto the sauce, and spread gently.

6. Sprinkle with mozzarella cheese, just enough to coat the layer.

7. Do two more layers of sauce, noodles, ricotta mixture, and mozzarella. End with another layer of noodles. Then spread more Zingy Red Sauce across the top. Sprinkle with remaining mozzarella and with the Parmesan.

8. Cover with foil and cook for 30–35 minutes. Then let stand 15 minutes before cutting and serving (or freezing).

Halibut Seared in Dill and Lemon

PREPARATION TIME: 15 MINUTES ♥ COOKING TIME: 6 MINUTES ♥ MAKES 2 SERVINGS

INGREDIENTS

1/2 CUP FRESH DILL LEAVES (OR 2 TBSP. DRIED, IF FRESH IS NOT AVAILABLE)

1/2 CUP FLAT LEAF PARSLEY

2 TBSP. CAPERS

2 TBSP. DIJON MUSTARD

2 TBSP. LEMON JUICE

2 TBSP. OLIVE OIL

SEA SALT AND BLACK PEPPER TO TASTE

1 LB. WHITEFISH, SUCH AS HALIBUT, COD, OR HADDOCK

COOKING SPRAY

1. Combine the dill, parsley, capers, mustard, lemon juice, oil, salt, and pepper. Using either a food processor or blender, process until finely chopped. (If you don't have either appliance, you can mash up the ingredients by hand with a fork; be sure to chop up the dill and parsley first, with a sharp knife. The result should be a chunky paste.)

2. Cut the fish into large, serving-size pieces (about the size of the palm of your hand), and coat with the dill paste.

3. Heat a nonstick frying pan over high heat. Coat with cooking spray or an additional tablespoon of olive oil. Add the fish and cook for 2–3 minutes per side, until the fish is browned and seared on the outside, and cooked through.

One of the very nicest things about life is the way we must regularly stop whatever it is we are doing and devote our attention to eating.

— LUCIANO PAVAROTTI AND WILLIAM WRIGHT
PAVAROTTI, MY OWN STORY

Sindbad Bars

Decadent. Addictive. Everything a dessert is meant to be. Sharing with the whole family will protect you from overindulgence.

PREPARATION TIME: 20 MINUTES ♥ COOKING TIME: 40–45 MINUTES ♥ MAKES 12 BARS

INGREDIENTS

1 CUP BUTTER ($^{1}/_{2}$ LB.)
4 OZ. UNSWEETENED CHOCOLATE
2 $^{1}/_{2}$ CUPS SUGAR
4 EGGS
1 CUP ALL-PURPOSE FLOUR
2 TSP. VANILLA
8 OZ. CREAM CHEESE, SOFTENED

TOPPING INGREDIENTS
1 CUP CHOCOLATE CHIPS (SEMI-SWEET)
2 TSP. VEGETABLE SHORTENING

1. Preheat oven to 350°. Grease a 9x13-inch pan.

2. Melt together the butter and unsweetened chocolate, either in a microwave or in the top of a double boiler. Cool slightly.

3. Using an electric mixer, thoroughly beat 2 cups of sugar and 3 of the eggs in a large mixing bowl. Stir in the flour and 1 tsp. of vanilla. Beat for 2 minutes at high speed. Slowly add the cooled chocolate and butter mix and blend completely.

4. In a food processor or a separate mixing bowl, combine cream cheese, $^{1}/_{2}$ cup sugar, 1 egg, and final teaspoon of vanilla. Process until smooth.

5. Spread the chocolate batter into the prepared pan. Drop the cream cheese mixture on top and spread to cover, being careful not to mix the batters. Bake until golden, 40–45 minutes. Place on rack to cool.

6. Once the bars are cooled, prepare the topping. Place the chocolate chips and vegetable shortening in a small heat-proof bowl and microwave for 1 minute. Stir until smooth. Decoratively drizzle the melted chocolate off the tines of a fork onto the cooled bars.

All you need is love. But a little chocolate now and then doesn't hurt.

— CHARLES M. SCHULZ

♥

All-American Chewy Chocolate Chip Cookies

Use an ice cream scoop to form the cookies, so you get a uniform size. If you under-cook them slightly, they'll stay chewy in the middle.

PREPARATION TIME: 15 MINUTES ♥ COOKING TIME: ABOUT 12 MINUTES
MAKES 12 LARGE COOKIES OR 24 SMALL ONES

INGREDIENTS

1 CUP SOFTENED BUTTER (^{1}/2 LB.)

3/4 CUP WHITE SUGAR

3/4 CUP LIGHT BROWN SUGAR

2 EGGS

1 TSP. VANILLA

2 ^{1}/2 CUPS ALL-PURPOSE FLOUR

1 TSP. BAKING SODA

2 CUPS CHOCOLATE CHIPS (SEMI-SWEET)

1. Preheat oven to 350°.

2. In a large mixing bowl, beat at high speed butter and white and brown sugars until light in color, about 3 minutes. Beat in eggs and vanilla until well blended. Slowly add flour and baking soda and beat until well mixed, about 2 minutes. Stir in chocolate chips until just combined.

3. Drop by teaspoon onto greased cookie sheet. Cook 10–12 minutes in preheated oven. Cool completely before devouring.

King Arthur Flour

One of my favorite cooking-related companies! It's been milling wheat since 1790 in Vermont, and today is employee-owned and environmentally sensitive. But more importantly, its products are pure—made without bleach, bromate, or other chemicals. I rely on the all-purpose variety in my recipes. (More baking tips to be found at www.kingarthurflour.com.)

Oatmeal Raisin Cookies

These are equally good with either raisins or chocolate chips.

PREPARATION TIME: 15 MINUTES ♥ COOKING TIME: ABOUT 12 MINUTES
MAKES 12 LARGE COOKIES OR 24 SMALL ONES

INGREDIENTS

1 CUP BUTTER	1 TBSP. MILK
1 1/4 CUPS BROWN SUGAR	3 CUPS OATMEAL
1/2 CUP WHITE SUGAR	1 1/2 CUPS ALL-PURPOSE FLOUR
2 EGGS	1 TSP. BAKING SODA
1 TSP. VANILLA	2 CUPS RAISINS

1. Preheat oven to 350°. Grease baking sheet.

2. Cream together butter and sugars, beating until they are light and fluffy.

3. Add eggs, vanilla, and milk, and continue beating until they are light.

4. Add oatmeal, flour, and baking soda and mix well. Stir in raisins.

5. Drop by large tablespoons on greased baking sheet. Cook for 10–12 minutes. Let cool a few minutes before removing from baking sheet.

Variation: For Oatmeal Chocolate Chip Cookies, substitute 2 cups chocolate chips for the raisins.

Cookies are made of butter and love.

— NORWEGIAN PROVERB

♥

Whoopie Pies

This Pennsylvania Dutch treat came to New England via a cookbook published by the creators of Marshmallow Fluff. It supposedly got its name because Amish children shouted "Whoopie!" when they found them in their school lunch sack.

PREPARATION TIME: 20 MINUTES ♥ COOKING TIME: 7–10 MINUTES ♥ MAKES 12 CAKES

INGREDIENTS

2 CUPS SUGAR

2 EGGS

2 TSP. VANILLA

1 TBSP. BAKING SODA

3/4 CUP UNSWEETENED DUTCH PROCESS COCOA POWDER

4 CUPS ALL-PURPOSE FLOUR

3/4 CUP BUTTER, SOFTENED

2 CUPS 2 PERCENT MILK

FILLING INGREDIENTS

1 CUP BUTTER, SOFTENED

2 CUPS POWDERED SUGAR, SIFTED

1 SMALL JAR (ABOUT 2 1/2 CUPS) MARSHMALLOW FLUFF

2 TSP. VANILLA

1. Preheat oven to 375°.

2. Cover two standard cookie sheets with parchment paper, or use nonstick but ungreased cookie sheets.

3. In mixer bowl, beat sugar, butter, eggs, and vanilla for about 3 minutes. In a separate bowl, combine baking soda, cocoa, and flour. Slowly add flour mixture to the butter-sugar mixture, alternating with the milk. Beat 3 minutes.

4. Drop cake batter by tablespoons onto prepared cookie sheets. There should be 30 cakes. Bake for 7–10 minutes until cakes spring back when lightly pressed. Cool completely.

5. For filling, beat the butter in a mixing bowl with an electric mixer until fluffy. Add the sifted powdered sugar, fluff, and vanilla. Beat until smooth. Spread between two cooled chocolate cakes.

I have this theory that chocolate slows down the aging process.... It may not be true, but do I dare take the chance?

— UNKNOWN

CHAPTER FIVE

The Dessert Table

"Stressed" spelled backwards
is "desserts." Coincidence?
I think not!

— AUTHOR UNKNOWN

Our Pie Pages →

A dessert made for sharing. Use a warm, sweet pie as your dinner-table centerpiece, and you'll have no problem getting the family to clean their plates.

AS A BONUS, PINWHEELS
Don't toss the excess pie crust. Roll it out again, sprinkle with cinnamon sugar and dot with butter. Then roll it up, slice into small pinwheels, and bake in the oven until brown. A perfect mini-treat while you're waiting for the pie to cool.

Perfect Pie Crust

This recipe works with both savory and sweet pies, and will make 2 single-crust pies or one two-crust pie (using a standard 9-inch pan).

PREPARATION TIME: 10 MINUTES   ♥   COOKING TIME: (DOUBLE CRUST) 50 MINUTES

INGREDIENTS

2 CUPS ALL-PURPOSE FLOUR

1/2 CUP (ABOUT 5 1/2 OZ.) COLD BUTTER CUT INTO CHUNKS

1/8 TSP. SALT

6–7 TBSP. ICE WATER

1. Put flour, butter, and salt in a food processor and pulse until butter is incorporated with the flour. (The mixture should be very finely grained.) Add water 1 Tbsp. at a time from the top, pulsing after each addition, until the flour forms a ball.*

2. Divide dough ball in half. (If making a single-crust pie, save remaining dough in the refrigerator, wrapped in plastic wrap, for up to 2 days.)

3. Generously flour your work surface and rolling pin. Take one dough ball and flatten it with the palm of your hand. Turn it over and flour the other side. Roll dough out from the center. Keep turning the dough over, to keep it covered with flour.

4. Roll the dough slightly larger than your pie pan.

5. Fold the rolled-out dough in half and gently transfer to the pie pan. Unfold it carefully and pat dough so that it conforms to the bottom and sides of the pie pan. (It should hang past the edges of the pan.) Trim the edges to 1/2-inch beyond the top of the pan, fold the edge under, and crimp slightly with a fork for an attractive edge.

*Note: If not using a food processor, combine salt and flour first. Cut butter into the flour with a pastry cutter until the mixture is finely grained. Add water 1 Tbsp. at a time, mixing water and flour together with a fork until it forms a ball.

Dot's Overstuffed Apple Pie

PREPARATION TIME: 20 MINUTES ♥ COOKING TIME: 50–60 MINUTES ♥ MAKES ONE 9–INCH PIE

INGREDIENTS

1 DOUBLE PIE CRUST, PREPARED

6–7 GRANNY SMITH APPLES, PEELED AND CUT INTO CHUNKS

1 CUP SUGAR, PLUS ADDITIONAL FOR SPRINKLING ON PIE CRUST

1/2 CUP ALL-PURPOSE FLOUR

1 TSP. CINNAMON

1/2 TSP. NUTMEG

1 TBSP. MILK

2 TBSP. BUTTER

1. Preheat oven to 375°.

2. Peel apples and cut into small chunks.

3. Put all ingredients except the butter into a large bowl. Mix well.

4. Pour the apple mixture into the prepared pie crust. Dot apples with 2 Tbsp. butter cut into small pieces.

5. Roll out top of pie crust, carefully placing it over the apples. Fold the top edges under the bottom edge of the crust, trimming excess. Using a fork or your fingers, make an edge. With a knife, make slits on top of the pie. Brush with milk over the top of the pie. Sprinkle with sugar.

6. Bake for about an hour until crust is gold-brown and apples are soft.

I don't think a really good pie can be made without a dozen or so children peeking over your shoulder as you stoop to look in at it every little while.

— JOHN GOULD

♥

Light as Heaven Lemon Meringue

PREPARATION TIME: 20 MINUTES ♥ COOKING TIME: 25 MINUTES ♥ MAKES ONE 9–INCH PIE

INGREDIENTS

1 CUP SUGAR

3 TBSP. CORNSTARCH

3 TBSP. ALL-PURPOSE FLOUR

1/4 TSP. SALT

1 1/4 CUP WATER

ZEST FROM 2 LEMONS

1/3 CUP FRESH LEMON JUICE

4 EGG YOLKS, BEATEN

2 TBSP. BUTTER

1 SINGLE 9-INCH PIE CRUST

1. Preheat oven to 350°

2. Cook pie crust in oven for 15 minutes or until lightly brown. (Follow instructions on page 78 and make one single pie crust.)

3. Combine sugar, cornstarch, flour, salt, and water in a saucepan, and place over high heat. Bring to a boil and stir until thickened, about 3 minutes. Combine the lemon zest and juice with the egg yolks. Slowly add the yolks to the hot sugar mixture, stirring constantly. Stir in butter, and cook for another 3 minutes. Transfer the hot lemon custard to the prepared pie crust. Top with meringue.

Meringue

INGREDIENTS

2 LARGE EGG WHITES

1/2 TSP. CREAM OF TARTAR

1/2 CUP SUGAR

1. Place the egg whites and cream of tartar in a clean bowl, and beat until they form soft peaks. Slowly add the sugar, while continuing to beat until the mixture forms stiff peaks. Spread meringue over the top of the pie, forming occasional peaks.

2. Bake the pie until the meringue browns slightly, about 10 minutes.

3. Let pie cool, then refrigerate for at least 2 hours before serving.

It is probable that the lemon is the most valuable of all fruit for preserving health.

— MAUD GRIEVE
A MODERN HERBAL (1971)

Easier-Than-You-Think Brownies

Why use a mix when it's so easy (and much cheaper) to whip these up "from scratch"?

PREPARATION TIME: 15 MINUTES ♥ COOKING TIME: 30–35 MINUTES ♥ MAKES 12 BROWNIES

INGREDIENTS

NON-STICK VEGETABLE SPRAY

3/4 CUP SEMI-SWEET CHOCOLATE CHIPS

3/4 CUP BUTTER

3 LARGE EGGS

1 CUP SUGAR

1/2 CUP LIGHTLY PACKED BROWN SUGAR

2 TBSP. CORN SYRUP

1 CUP ALL-PURPOSE FLOUR

1 TSP. BAKING POWDER

1/4 TSP. SALT

1 CUP WALNUTS

1. Preheat oven to 350°.

2. Coat a 9x13-inch baking pan with nonstick vegetable spray.

3. Melt the chocolate and butter in a pan on the stove or in a bowl in the microwave. In a large bowl, mix eggs, sugar, brown sugar, and corn syrup until blended. Stir in the chocolate mixture.

4. In a separate bowl, stir the flour, baking powder, and salt together with a fork. Stir into the egg mixture. Add the nuts, and stir to evenly distribute.

5. Bake for 30–35 minutes.

6. Cool before cutting.

Note: Be sure not to overmix or overcook the batter, and the brownies will come out chewy and delicious.

ALTERNATIVE BIRTHDAY CAKE

If your family chocoholic has a birthday, consider a "brownie buffet" instead of the traditional cake. Bake up the brownies, and set out an array of topping—ice cream, whipped cream, hot fudge, caramel, multicolored sprinkles—and a candle for each brownie.

Lemon Squares

Sweet for kids, tangy enough for adults, luscious, and light. A perfect accompaniment to a summertime dinner on the back porch.

PREPARATION TIME: 15 MINUTES ♥ COOKING TIME: 30–35 MINUTES ♥ MAKES 12 SQUARES

INGREDIENTS

FOR CRUST

2 CUPS ALL-PURPOSE FLOUR

1/2 CUP POWDERED SUGAR

1 CUP BUTTER, COLD AND CUT INTO SMALL CHUNKS

MORE POWDERED SUGAR FOR SPRINKLING AT THE END

INGREDIENTS FOR FILLING

4 EGGS

ZEST OF 2 MEDIUM LEMONS

1 1/2 CUPS SUGAR

1/4 CUP ALL-PURPOSE FLOUR

1 TSP. BAKING POWDER

1/3–1/2 CUP FRESH LEMON JUICE

1. Preheat oven to 350°. Grease a 9x13-inch pan.

2. In a food processor or with a pastry cutter, combine flour and powered sugar. Add the butter chunks and pulse with the processor or cut into until the mixture resembles coarse crumbs. Reserve 1/3 cup of the mixture.

3. Press the remaining crumbs into the prepared pan. Bake for 10–15 minutes, until lightly browned at the edges.

4. While the base is baking, prepare the filling. Beat the eggs and lemon zest with a mixer. Add the sugar, flour, baking powder, and lemon juice. Beat all ingredients until well combined.

5. Pour the filling mix over the hot base. Sprinkle the reserved crumbs over the top. Return to the oven and bake until golden, about 20 minutes.

6. When cooled, sprinkle with powdered sugar and cut into squares.

Bringing up a family should be an adventure, not an anxious discipline in which everybody is constantly graded for performance.

— MILTON R. SAPIRSTEIN

Raspberry Lemon Parfait

MAKES 4 SERVINGS

INGREDIENTS

8 OZ. WHIPPING CREAM

1 TBSP. SUGAR

$^1/_2$ TSP. LEMON ZEST

2 CUPS FRESH RASPBERRIES

4 PARFAIT GLASSES OR SOME OTHER TYPE OF TALL GLASS

1. First make the whipping cream. Place cream in bowl of an electric mixer equipped with whisk attachment. Slowly start to beat, then increase speed to high. After a few minutes, stop mixer and add the sugar and lemon zest. Continue to beat until stiff peaks form. Don't overbeat.

2. In the parfait glasses, layer the raspberries and whipped cream, starting with raspberries on the bottom, and ending with whipped cream. On top of the whipped cream, put a raspberry.

Raspberry Turnovers

Let the kids cut the circles from the pie crust dough with the lid from a quart-sized container of yogurt or sour cream.

PREPARATION TIME: 15 MINUTES ♥ COOKING TIME: 15 MINUTES ♥ MAKES 12 TURNOVERS

INGREDIENTS

1 DOUBLE BASIC PIE CRUST (RECIPE, PAGE 78)

1 CUP RASPBERRY PRESERVES

2 TBSP. MILK

2 TBSP. SUGAR

1. Preheat oven to 350°. Lightly grease cookie sheet or cover with parchment paper.

2. Roll out half the dough at a time on a floured board. Roll the dough thin.

3. Cut 5 circles (about 6 inches in diameter) from each half of dough.

4. Place each circle on the cookie sheet and put 1 Tbsp. of preserves in the center of the circle. Fold over the edges until they meet. Crimp edges with a fork, and prick the top a few times with the fork.

5. Continue until all dough is used.

6. Using a pastry brush, brush the tops with the milk, then sprinkle with sugar.

7. Bake until lightly browned, about 15 minutes. Cool completely.

Amish Cocoa Squares

Experimenting is part of the pleasure in cooking. The Boston Globe printed this basic recipe 35 years ago; I added the chocolate chips (a bit more chocolate never hurts).

PREPARATION TIME: 20 MINUTES ♥ COOKING TIME: 25–30 MINUTES ♥ MAKES 12 SQUARES

INGREDIENTS

1 CUP OATS

1 1/2 CUPS HOT WATER

1 1/2 CUPS SUGAR

1/2 CUP COCOA

1/2 CUP BUTTER, SOFTENED

2 EGGS

1 TSP. VANILLA

1 1/2 CUPS ALL-PURPOSE FLOUR

1 1/2 TSP. BAKING SODA

1 CUP CHOCOLATE CHIPS

POWDERED SUGAR

1. Preheat oven to 350°. Grease a 9x13-inch pan.

2. In a mixing bowl, stir oats and hot water together. Cool to room temperature, about 10 minutes. Mix in sugar, cocoa, butter, and eggs. Stir in vanilla. Slowly add the flour and baking soda. Beat well. Stir in chocolate chips.

3. Pour into a prepared pan. Bake until a toothpick inserted comes out clean, about 25–30 minutes. Cool. Dust with powdered sugar, and cut into squares.

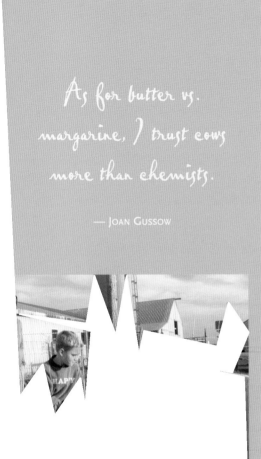

Blueberry Cream Cheese Bars

PREPARATION TIME: 15 MINUTES ♥ COOKING TIME: 50 MINUTES ♥ MAKES 24 BARS

INGREDIENTS

HOT SHORTBREAD BASE (RECIPE BELOW)
16 OZ. CREAM CHEESE, SOFTENED
2 LARGE EGGS

3/4 CUP SUGAR
1 TSP. VANILLA
3/4 CUP FRESH OR FROZEN BLUEBERRIES

1. Preheat oven to 350°.

2. Grease a 9x13-inch baking pan.

3. In a bowl, whisk cream cheese until smooth, then whisk in eggs, sugar, and vanilla. Spread blueberries evenly over hot shortbread, and pour cream cheese mixture over it.

4. Bake until slightly puffed, about 30 minutes. Cool completely in pan, and cut into bars.

5. Bar cookies keep, covered and chilled, for 3 days.

Hot Shortbread Base

INGREDIENTS

3/4 CUP BUTTER
2 CUPS ALL-PURPOSE FLOUR

1/2 CUP BROWN SUGAR

♥ In a food processor, process all ingredients until the mixture forms small lumps. Press into a 9x13 pan. Bake for about 20 minutes or until light brown.

Carrot Cake with Cream Cheese Frosting

PREPARATION TIME: 20 MINUTES ♥ COOKING TIME: 35–40 MINUTES

INGREDIENTS

2 CUPS ALL-PURPOSE FLOUR, SIFTED

1 TSP. BAKING SODA

1 TSP. BAKING POWDER

1 1/2 TSP. CINNAMON

1/2 TSP. SALT

2 CUPS WHITE SUGAR

1 1/2 CUPS VEGETABLE OIL

4 EGGS

3 CUPS CARROTS, FINELY GRATED*

1. Preheat oven to 350°. Grease a 9x13-inch baking pan.**

2. Sift together the flour, baking soda, baking powder, cinnamon, and salt, and set aside.

3. In a large mixing bowl, combine the sugar and oil. Add the eggs, one at a time, beating well after each addition.

4. Gradually add dry ingredients, beating just until combined. Gently fold in grated carrots.

5. Pour into prepared pan and bake for 35–40 minutes.

6. Let cool, then top with icing (see mini-recipe).

*Time-Saving Tip: In many supermarkets, you can find packages of grated carrots.

**Note: This cake can be made into a double-layer cake using two round cake pans. Reduce baking time to 25–30 minutes, or until a tester inserted into center of cake comes out clean.

A MINI RECIPE

Icing for Carrot Cake

INGREDIENTS

1/4 CUP BUTTER, SOFTENED

1 (8 OZ.) PACKAGE CREAM CHEESE, SOFTENED

3 CUPS POWDERED SUGAR

2 TSP. VANILLA

♥ Using an electric mixer, cream butter and cream cheese together. Gradually add the powdered sugar and beat well. Add the vanilla, stirring just enough to blend.

Iced Mocha with Whipped Cream

Delicious on a hot summer's day.

PREP TIME: 3 MINUTES
MAKES 1 SERVING

INGREDIENTS

ICE CUBES

4 OZ. ESPRESSO OR 8 OZ. STRONG BLACK COFFEE, COOLED

2% MILK, ENOUGH TO ALMOST FILL GLASS

2 GOOD SQUIRTS CHOCOLATE SYRUP

1 16-OZ. GLASS

WHIPPED CREAM

CHOCOLATE SHAVINGS

1. Put ice cubes, espresso or coffee, milk, and chocolate syrup in the glass. Using a spoon, stir to mix all ingredients. Taste to make sure you have enough chocolate.
2. Put whipped cream on top, and the chocolate shavings on top of the whipped cream. Enjoy!

Dr. Wheeler's Congo Bars

My dentist, Dr. Wheeler, didn't invent these bars, but I'm naming them after him anyway. In the summer, when the line's out the door at Espresso Love, as soon as Dr. Wheeler catches my eye he calls out: "Got the Congo Bars today?" Almost every morning he's on-Island he buys two, and an Iced Mocha, and eats them on the dock by the Yacht Club. Good thing he's a swimmer, biker, and dentist.

PREPARATION TIME: 15 MINUTES ♥ COOKING TIME: 30–35 MINUTES ♥ MAKES 12 BARS

INGREDIENTS

1 CUP BUTTER ($^1/_2$ LB.)

$^3/_4$ CUP WHITE SUGAR

$^3/_4$ CUP BROWN SUGAR

2 EGGS

1 TSP. VANILLA EXTRACT

2$^1/_4$ CUPS ALL-PURPOSE FLOUR

1 TSP. BAKING SODA

2 CUPS SEMI-SWEET CHOCOLATE CHIPS

1. Preheat over to 350°.

2. Grease a 9x13-inch pan.

3. Beat butter and sugars at medium speed with an electric mixer for 3 minutes. Scrape the bowl, then add eggs and vanilla and beat another 3 minutes, occasionally scraping the sides and bottom of the bowl.

4. Slowly add flour and baking soda. Beat two minutes.

5. Add chocolate chips, stirring on low or by hand.

6. Evenly spread the dough in the greased pan. Cook for 30–35 minutes. The bars should be chewy.

Variations: Add nuts and/or substitute other kinds of chips for the chocolate chips.

Two Quick Breads →

You can also make these breads in a mini-loaf pan and wrap them up with a pretty ribbon and give them as gifts at the holidays.

Banana Bread

PREPARATION TIME: 15 MINUTES ♥ COOKING TIME: 50 MINUTES ♥ MAKES 1 LOAF

INGREDIENTS

$^1/_2$ CUP SHORTENING

1 CUP SUGAR

3 LARGE RIPE BANANAS, MASHED

2 EGGS, BEATEN

$^3/_4$ TSP. BAKING SODA

2 CUPS ALL-PURPOSE FLOUR

$^1/_2$ TSP. SALT

1 TBSP. CINNAMON

1 CUP WALNUTS, CHOPPED

1. Preheat oven to 350°. Grease a loaf pan.

2. Cream shortening and sugar in a large bowl. Add mashed bananas and eggs, then sifted dry ingredients and walnuts.

3. Bake for 50 minutes or until a tester comes out clean. Cool before slicing.

Cranberry-Orange Bread

PREPARATION TIME: 20 MINUTES ♥ COOKING TIME: 60–70 MINUTES ♥ MAKES 2 LOAVES

INGREDIENTS

4 CUPS ALL-PURPOSE FLOUR

2 CUPS SUGAR

4 TSP. BAKING POWDER

1 TSP. BAKING SODA

1/2 CUP COLD BUTTER, CUT INTO PIECES

2 EGGS, BEATEN

2 TBSP. ORANGE ZEST

1 1/2 CUPS ORANGE JUICE

3 CUPS FRESH CRANBERRIES, CHOPPED

1. Preheat oven to 350°.

2. Grease two loaf pans.

3. Place flour, sugar, baking powder, baking soda, and butter in a food processor and pulse until butter is combined and there are small granules. (Alternatively, use a pastry cutter to cut butter into dry ingredients.)

4. Pour into a large bowl and stir in eggs, orange zest, and orange juice until just combined. Add cranberries to the mix.

5. Pour into greased loaf pans and bake at least 60 minutes or until a toothpick inserted in the middle comes out clean.

A Case for All-Purpose Flour

Flour comes in a wide variety of types. The recipes I use in this book call for all-purpose flour, and (as I state on page 73) I strongly recommend the King Arthur's brand. A look at the most common types of flour:

ALL-PURPOSE FLOUR: Very finely textured, it works in most recipes. "Stone-ground" on the package means the flour was ground between stones, crushing the grain without generating the heat commercial steel grinders make, which strips away nutrients. If possible choose unbleached all-purpose flour—although some flour companies use a natural bleaching process, many use chemicals.

BREAD FLOUR: An unbleached, high-gluten flour ideal for yeast breads.

CAKE FLOUR: Fine-textured, and excellent for cakes and pastry.

WHOLE-WHEAT FLOUR: The most nutritious flour, because it retains the wheat germ, which means it has high fiber content. You can substitute up to 25 per cent of a recipe's flour with whole-wheat, without significantly altering the texture.

Chapter Six

The World's Table

What is patriotism but the
love of the food one ate
as a child?

— LIN YUTANG

WHEN YOU TRAVEL and enjoy a special dish, don't hesitate to ask for the recipe. Back home it will inspire memories of a wonderful trip for you and your family.

Theo the Greek's Spinach Pie

While at a workshop for women on the Greek island of Hydra, I had dinner every night at the local tavern. The owner, Theo, was handsome, with big, dark eyes. One night I asked if could cook with him; he showed me how to make this savory pie.

PREPARATION TIME: 20 MINUTES ♥ COOKING TIME: 35–40 MINUTES ♥ SERVES 6–8

INGREDIENTS

1 TBSP. CHOPPED GARLIC

3 TBSP. OLIVE OIL (HAVE MORE ON HAND, IF NEEDED, FOR SAUTÉING)

12 OZ. DEFROSTED CHOPPED SPINACH, WITH LIQUID SQUEEZED OUT

2 CUPS CANNED WHOLE TOMATOES, DRAINED AND CHOPPED INTO LARGE PIECES (YOU CAN USE THE EQUIVALENT AMOUNT IN FRESH TOMATOES)

$^1/_4$ TSP. GROUND BLACK PEPPER

$^1/_4$ TSP. GROUND NUTMEG

4 EGGS, LIGHTLY WHISKED TOGETHER

9 OZ. FETA CHEESE, CRUMBLED INTO SMALL CHUNKS

BASIC PIE CRUST FOR SINGLE PIE (RECIPE, PAGE 78)

1. Preheat oven to 350°.

2. In a frying pan, sauté garlic in olive oil over low heat for 2 minutes. Add defrosted spinach drained of liquid. Sauté for 3 more minutes. Add chopped tomatoes, pepper, and nutmeg, and sauté 2 more minutes. Set vegetables aside to cool.

3. In a large bowl, whisk eggs. Add cooled vegetables. Fold in feta cheese, and pour into prepared pie crust.

4. Bake pie 35–40 minutes until firm in center.

Greek Stuffed Aubergine

PREPARATION TIME: 20 MINUTES ♥ COOKING TIME: 30 MINUTES ♥ SERVES 4

INGREDIENTS

3 OR 4 SMALL, LONG AUBERGINES (EGG-PLANTS), ABOUT 2 LBS., STEMS DISCARDED (USE THE LONG, THIN "ASIAN" EGGPLANT, NOT THE CHUBBY OBLONG TYPE)

2 TBSP. SALT

4 TBSP. OLIVE OIL

1 LARGE ONION, CHOPPED

2 TBSP. MINCED GARLIC

2 FRESH TOMATOES, CUT UP AND PEELED

3 TBSP. PARSLEY

SALT AND PEPPER, FRESHLY GROUND

1/2 CUP PARMESAN CHEESE, GRATED

1. Preheat oven to 350°.

2. Cut open eggplants length-wise and sprinkle salt on them. Let stand for half an hour, then squeeze all the water out and rinse them.

3. Put 2 Tbsp. olive oil in frying pan, and fry eggplants on both sides until they soften.

4. Take them out of pan, add more olive oil and sauté onion and garlic until clear. Add tomatoes and cook until softened. Add parsley, and salt and pepper to taste.

5. Stuff the ingredients into the eggplant, place in a baking dish or pan. Put a half a cup of water into pan to prevent eggplant from drying out or sticking. Bake for 30 minutes at 350°. Sprinkle cheese on top after baking.

A meal shared by friends and family is one of the bonding rituals without which the family, society even, can fall apart.

— ANTONIA TILL

Sweet & Sour Pork

I took a Chinese cooking class on Martha's Vineyard, and the teacher handed out several recipes. Rice is a good accompaniment to this dish.

PREPARATION TIME: 30 MINUTES ♥ COOKING TIME: 20 MINUTES ♥ SERVES 4

INGREDIENTS

1 LB. PORK TENDERLOIN

2 GREEN PEPPERS, CUT INTO 1-INCH SQUARES

1 SMALL CAN PINEAPPLE CHUNKS

3 CUPS VEGETABLE OIL

$1/2$ CUP CORNSTARCH

PORK MARINADE INGREDIENTS

$1/2$ TSP. SALT

$1/2$ TBSP. SOY SAUCE

1 TBSP. CORNSTARCH

1 TBSP. COLD WATER

1 EGG YOLK

SEASONING SAUCE INGREDIENTS

3 TBSP. RICE VINEGAR

4 TBSP. SUGAR

4 TBSP. CATSUP

5 TBSP. COLD WATER

3 TSP. CORNSTARCH

1 TSP. SALT

1 TSP. SESAME OIL

1 TSP. GROUND GINGER

1 TSP. GARLIC, CHOPPED

2 SCALLIONS, CHOPPED

1. Mix up the Pork Marinade and set aside.

2. Mix up the Seasoning Sauce and set aside.

3. Pound the pork with the back of a cleaver to tenderize it. Cut into 1-inch squares. Marinate for at least 30 minutes.

4. Meanwhile, cut green pepper into halves, remove seeds and membranes, and slice into 1-inch squares. Set aside.

5. Heat 3 cups oil. While oil is heating, remove pork from marinated and coat each piece in $1/2$ cup cornstarch. When the oil is hot, fry pork in batches until brown and

done, about 2 minutes. When all the pork is fried, reheat the oil and fry the meat again until crispy, 2 or 3 minutes more.

6. Remove heat and drain oil from frying pan, leaving in 2 Tbsp.

7. Reheat the oil and fry green pepper and pineapple, stirring constantly. Add the seasoning sauce, continuing to stir fry until it is thickened. Turn off heat. Add the pork, mix well, and serve immediately.

Fennel, Pear, and Parmesan Salad

Michael Altman, a British chef and bed-and-breakfast owner in France, created this recipe. He serves it with grilled steak.

PREPARATION TIME: 10 MINUTES   ♥   SERVES 6

INGREDIENTS

2 BULBS FENNEL

2 RIPE PEARS

COARSELY MILLED BLACK PEPPER

OLIVE OIL

FRESH GRATED PARMESAN CHEESE

1. Remove the feathery tops from the fennel. Roughly chop the tops and set aside.

2. Cut the rest of the fennel into wafer thin slices; arrange on a serving platter.

3. Slice the pears and scatter over the fennel with lots of pepper. Drizzle with olive oil.

4. Using a potato peeler, pare the Parmesan over the top of the fennel, then scatter the chopped fennel tops over all and serve.

A family in harmony will prosper in everything.

— CHINESE PROVERB

Greek Salad

Making native dishes can teach a lot about a place. For instance, lettuce doesn't grow well on the rocky island of Hydra, so the salad I got at the local taverna featured this mix of vegetables, without a green leaf in sight.

PREPARATION TIME: 10 MINUTES ♥ SERVES 4

INGREDIENTS

6 LARGE RIPE TOMATOES (PLUM OR HEIRLOOM), CUT INTO MEDIUM CHUNKS

1 SMALL CUCUMBER

4 OZ. GREEK OLIVES

FRESH OR DRIED BASIL (IF FRESH, CUT IN RIBBONS)

6 OZ. FETA CHEESE

A FEW SLICES OF RED ONION

SALT AND FRESH PEPPER TO TASTE

3 TBSP. EXTRA-VIRGIN OLIVE OIL

♥ In a medium bowl, place all the ingredients. Toss lightly. Lightly pour olive oil over salad and toss again.

Classic Tapenade on Pita Crisps

Classic Tapenade is a thick paste of olives and seasoning, from the Provençal region of France, but it can be made with other vegetables (see Roasted Red Pepper Tapenade, page 68). Use tapenade to dress up a sandwich or as a spread on crackers or crusty bread, or include it on a platter of appetizers, along with baby carrots, celery, and cubes of ham and cheese.

PREPARATION TIME: 20 MINUTES ♥ SERVES 8

INGREDIENTS

¹/₂ LB. GOOD BLACK GREEK OLIVES, PITTED AND DICED

1 CLOVE GARLIC, MINCED

¹/₂ CUP EXTRA VIRGIN OLIVE OIL

1 TBSP. LEMON JUICE

1 TSP. MINCED FRESH THYME LEAVES

1 RECIPE PITA CRISPS

1. Put all the ingredients in a food processor and blend until slightly smooth.

2. Serve on Pita Crisps (see mini-recipe).

A MINI RECIPE

Pita Crisps

COOKING TIME: 10 MINUTES

INGREDIENTS

2 WHOLE PITAS

3 TBSP. OLIVE OIL

SALT AND PEPPER

1. Preheat oven to 375°.

2. Cut pitas into quarters. Put pita on a cookie sheet and brush with olive oil. Lightly salt and pepper. Cook for about 10 minutes. Cool and serve with the tapenade.

English Shepherd Pie

An authentic English dish, from my south-of-London friend, Peta.

PREPARATION TIME: 20 MINUTES ♥ COOKING TIME: 25 MINUTES ♥ SERVES 8

INGREDIENTS

1 TBSP. OLIVE OIL

1 SMALL ONION, DICED

2 GARLIC CLOVES, MINCED

1 CUP SLICED BUTTON MUSHROOMS

2 LBS. GROUND BEEF

1/2 CUP SLICED CARROTS

1/2 CUP FROZEN PEAS

1/2 CUP FROZEN CORN

2 BEEF BOUILLON CUBES

2 TBSP. WORCESTERSHIRE SAUCE

1/2 CUP CANNED WHOLE PLUM TOMATOES

1 TSP. SALT

FRESHLY GROUND PEPPER

6 IDAHO POTATOES, COOKED AND PEELED

2 TBSP. BUTTER

1/2 CUP MILK

1. Preheat oven to 350°.

2. In a large skillet, sauté onion, garlic, and mushrooms for about 5 minutes. Add the ground beef, carrots, peas, corn, bouillon cubes, Worcestershire sauce, and tomatoes. Add salt and pepper. Cook until ground beef is browned, about 10 minutes. Pour into a 9x13-inch glass dish.

3. Put peeled potatoes, butter, milk, and salt and pepper to taste into the bowl of an electric mixer. Beat at high speed until smooth. Spread on top of ground beef mixture.

4. Bake in oven about 20–25 minutes or until potatoes are slightly browned on top.

French Pear Clafouti

Clafouti is a sweet fruit baked in a batter—a south of France classic. Any type of apple works, as well as pears; the key to success is keeping flour to a minimum and making sure the oven is preheated.

PREPARATION TIME: 20 MINUTES ♥ COOKING TIME: 35 MINUTES ♥ MAKES 1 10–INCH TART

INGREDIENTS

NONSTICK COOKING SPRAY

2 CUPS CUBED PEELED PEARS OR APPLES

3/4 CUP ALL-PURPOSE FLOUR, PLUS 1 TSP.

1/4 TSP. SALT

1/8 TSP. NUTMEG

2 CUPS 2 PERCENT MILK

4 LARGE EGGS, LIGHTLY BEATEN

1/2 CUP SUGAR

1/2 TSP. VANILLA EXTRACT

1. Preheat oven to 375°.

2. Coat a 10-inch deep-dish pie plate with cooking spray, then dust with 1 tsp. flour.

3. Arrange the pear cubes in the bottom of the prepared dish and set aside.

4. Combine remaining 3/4 cup flour, salt, and nutmeg in a bowl. Gradually add 1 cup milk, stirring with a whisk until well-blended. Add second cup of milk, eggs, sugar, and vanilla extract, stirring until smooth. Pour batter over pear cubes.

5. Bake for 35 minutes or until set. This can be eaten either while still hot or at room temperature, and served with whipped cream or vanilla ice cream.

Table Talk Conversation Starters

HOLIDAY WISH LIST

Make December dinners a time for a Wish List Review. Each night one family member gets the chance to tell us his or her top-five wishes for the holiday season . . . whether it's world peace, an idea for a family project to cut waste, or a yen for the latest iPod.

Venetian Shrimp Risotto

PREPARATION TIME: 20 MINUTES ♥ COOKING TIME: 30 MINUTES ♥ SERVES 4

INGREDIENTS

2 TBSP. OLIVE OIL

1 ONION, DICED

1 CUP ARBORIO RICE

1 CUP WHITE WINE

2 CUPS CHICKEN STOCK

2 TBSP. BUTTER

$^1/_4$ CUP FRESHLY GRATED PARMESAN CHEESE

2 TBSP. HEAVY CREAM

1 LB. MEDIUM-SIZE SHRIMP, SHELLED AND DEVEINED

FOR PREPARING SHRIMP:

1 ADDITIONAL TBSP. OLIVE OIL

FRESH THYME, FRESH ROSEMARY CHOPPED SMALL

1. Heat chicken stock to boiling point, then have it ready at stoveside.

2. Sauté shrimp in olive oil and herbs.

3. Using a large skillet, heat 2 Tbsp. olive oil, and sauté the onions until they are clear in color, being careful not to brown them.

4. Add the Arborio rice, stir to coat with olive oil, and sauté with the onions to toast each grain of rice, about 7 minutes.

5. Once the rice is lightly basted, add the white wine slowly, stirring with a wooden spoon so the rice is not damaged.

6. After the rice has absorbed the white wine and the skillet is nearly dry, add 1 cup stock, stirring occasionally, and cook over very low heat until stock is absorbed. Add the rest of the stock until it, too, is absorbed. This will take about 17–20 minutes.

7. After all of the liquid has been added and the rice is chewy yet fully cooked, with a creamy texture, add the butter, Parmesan, and heavy cream. Stir to combine. Add sautéed shrimp. Serve immediately.

On a January Saturday night I was in a café on the Venetian lagoon island of Burano. As I enjoyed this risotto I watched through the window as families of the town, all dressed up, strolled down the street, visiting with each other. Neighbors and friends shared stories, laughed, and exchanged news. Every Saturday night, I learned, is family night in Burano. Wouldn't it be great if American towns had a tradition like this?

Focaccia Bread

I'm often asked if it's "worth it" to make your own bread. Focaccia is; freshness is crucial (the store-bought versions are almost always too tough), and the leftovers can be used for a special grilled cheese sandwich the next day.

PREPARATION TIME: 2 ¹/₂ HOURS ♥ COOKING TIME: 25 MINUTES

INGREDIENTS

¹/₂ OZ. DRY YEAST

1³/₄ CUP WARM WATER

¹/₂ TBSP. SUGAR

¹/₄ CUP MILK

3/₄ CUP OLIVE OIL

4 CUPS ALL-PURPOSE FLOUR

CORNMEAL

1 TBSP. SALT, PLUS MORE TO SPRINKLE ON TOP

¹/₂ TBSP. PEPPER

1 TBSP. FRESH ROSEMARY, MINCED

¹/₂ CUP MORE OLIVE OIL FOR TOP OF BREAD

1. Put yeast, 1 cup warm water, and sugar into a large mixing bowl that will fit a mixer equipped with a dough hook. Let sit for about 10 minutes, until yeast is creamy. Add the rest of the water and milk.

2. Mix at low speed for about 2 minutes. Add the olive oil and mix for 1 minute.

3. Slowly add the flour, mixing in between each addition of flour. Add the salt to the last batch of flour. Put dough into large greased bowl and place a wet dish towel on top.

4. Let the dough rise for 1 ¹/₂ hours. Punch down dough, then spread dough on a cookie sheet that has been sprinkled with cornmeal. Let the dough rise for another half an hour.

5. Preheat oven to 425°.

6. Make indentations on top of raised dough. Fill with ¹/₂ cup olive oil. Sprinkle salt, pepper, and fresh rosemary on top. Put in oven and bake until golden brown, about 25 minutes.

♥ *Let the kids mix the water, sugar, and yeast and watch for the "foaming action" that tells you it's ready for the next step.*

Tomato, Basil, Mozzarella, and Prosciutto Focaccia Sandwich with Balsamic Roasted Onions

This can either be a sandwich or a salad, with bread on the side. If you decide to make a salad, layer the ingredients on a salad plate and drizzle with olive oil.

PREPARATION TIME: 10 MINUTES ♥ COOKING TIME: 20 MINUTES ♥ MAKES 2 SANDWICHES

INGREDIENTS

2 MEDIUM RED ONIONS, THINLY SLICED

$^1/_2$ CUP BALSAMIC VINEGAR

4 TBSP. OLIVE OIL

$^1/_4$ LB. PROSCIUTTO, THINLY SLICED

2 ROMA TOMATOES, SLICED

$^1/_4$ CUP FRESH BASIL LEAVES

$^1/_2$ LB. FRESH MOZZARELLA

SALT AND FRESHLY GROUND PEPPER

FOCACCIA BREAD

1. Preheat oven to 350°.

2. Spread onions sliced evenly on a cookie sheet. Pour balsamic vinegar over onions, stirring to coat evenly. Bake for about 20 minutes. Remove from oven and cool.

3. Slice piece of focaccia and cut in half. Brush olive oil on both sides of bread. Layer prosciutto, tomato, basil leaves, mozzarella, and the baked onions between the slices. Salt and pepper to taste.

It has been well said that a hungry man is more interested in four sandwiches than four freedoms.

— HENRY CABOT LODGE, JR.

Brazilian Potato Salad

Maria Fatima Souza, a longtime Espresso Love employee, makes this for the café every week. The carrots add both flavor and color, and the egg a bit of protein.

PREPARATION TIME: 20 MINUTES ♥ COOKING TIME: 30 MINUTES ♥ MAKES 6 SERVINGS

INGREDIENTS

4 LARGE IDAHO POTATOES, UNPEELED

1 1/2 MEDIUM CARROTS, WITH TOP OFF AND PEELED

1 MEDIUM ONION CUT INTO QUARTERS

3 HARD-BOILED EGGS

SALT AND PEPPER TO TASTE

1 CUP MAYONNAISE

1 1/2 FRESH PLUM TOMATOES, PEELED, SEEDED, AND CUT INTO SMALL CHUNKS

1. Cook potatoes, carrots, and onion in a large pot of water until potatoes are soft. Take out of pot and cool.

2. While the vegetables are cooking, cook the eggs until hard boiled. Let them cool.

3. Peel the potatoes. Cut potatoes, carrots, and onions into small chunks. Put into a large bowl. Cut cooled eggs into small pieces and add to vegetables. Salt and pepper to taste. Add the mayonnaise, mixing gently. Add the plum tomato chunks and toss lightly.

Turkey Tacos

PREPARATION TIME: 20 MINUTES ♥ COOKING TIME: 25 MINUTES ♥ SERVES 4

INGREDIENTS

2 TBSP. CANOLA OIL

1 LB. GROUND TURKEY

1 SMALL ONION, CHOPPED

1/2 GREEN PEPPER, CHOPPED

2 CLOVE GARLIC, MINCED

1 TBSP. CHILI POWDER

1 TSP. DRIED OREGANO

1/2 TSP. CUMIN

1 (15 OZ.) CAN KIDNEY BEANS, RINSED AND DRAINED

1 (8 OZ.) CAN TOMATO SAUCE

TACO SHELLS (HARD OR SOFT)

2 CUPS SHREDDED LETTUCE

2 PLUM TOMATOES DICED INTO SMALL PIECES

2 CUPS GRATED CHEDDAR CHEESE

2 CUPS STORE-BOUGHT SALSA

1. Heat oil in large frying pan. Add ground turkey and sauté for 6 minutes or until thoroughly cooked. Add the onion, green pepper, garlic, chili powder, oregano, and cumin. Continue to cook 5 minutes longer.

2. Drain fat from pan. Add beans and tomato sauce. Simmer for about 18 minutes. The mixture should be slightly thick.

3. Serve in taco shells with shredded lettuce, diced tomato, grated cheddar, and salsa.

Food is our common ground, a universal experience.

— JAMES BEARD

♥

Virgin Island Key Lime Pie

This recipe comes from the chef at the Sandcastle, on tiny Jost Van Dyke in the British Virgin Islands. Serve it on a warm summer night . . . or on a cold night when you're yearning for the Caribbean. If key limes are unavailable, regular limes will do.

PREPARATION TIME: 15 MINUTES ♥ BAKING TIME: 20–25 MINUTES, PLUS BROWNING TIME
MAKES 1 9-INCH PIE

INGREDIENTS

SINGLE 9-INCH BASIC PIE CRUST (RECIPE, PAGE 78)

14 OZ. SWEETENED CONDENSED MILK

6 EGG YOLKS

DASH OF SALT

$^1/2$ CUP KEY LIME JUICE

2 TBSP. KEY LIME ZEST

1 TBSP. ORANGE ZEST

1. Preheat oven to 350°.

2. Bake pie crust in oven for 10–15 minutes. Cool completely.

3. Meanwhile, beat condensed milk, eggs, and salt together. Add juice and zest. Pour into cooled pie shell and bake 10 minutes.

4. Top with meringue (recipe, page 80).

I was 32 when I started cooking; up until then, I just ate.

— JULIA CHILD

Moroccan Lamb Kabobs with Rice

Serving meat on a skewer always ups the fun in dinner. This dish has some surprising spices, but it's sweet and mild and perfect for a family meal.

PREPARATION TIME: 12 HOURS   ♥   COOKING TIME: 20 MINUTES   ♥   SERVES 6

INGREDIENTS

2 MEDIUM ONIONS, CHOPPED

$^2/_3$ CUP LEMON JUICE

6 TBSP. OLIVE OIL

2 TSP. SALT

1$^1/_2$ TSP. DRIED THYME, CRUSHED

$^1/_2$ TSP. FRESHLY GROUND PEPPER

3 LBS. BONELESS LEG OF LAMB, CUT INTO 1-INCH CUBES

2 CLOVES GARLIC, MINCED

1. Make a marinade by combining onion, garlic, lemon juice, olive oil, salt, thyme, and pepper. Add lamb, cover, and refrigerate several hours or overnight.

2. Drain meat, reserving marinade.

3. Thread meat on skewers. Grill over medium coals or medium heat on a gas grill about 20 minutes, brushing with marinade and turning skewers often.

4. Serve with rice.

Variation: You can add green peppers and red peppers to the skewers. Cut them into 1$^1/_2$-inch pieces. You can also add mushrooms.

A MINI RECIPE

Moroccan Rice

PREP TIME: 10 MINUTES
COOKING TIME: 30 MINUTES
MAKES 6 SERVINGS

INGREDIENTS

$^1/_4$ CUP OLIVE OIL

1 SMALL ONION, DICED

1 CLOVE GARLIC, MINCED

2 CUPS LONG-GRAIN WHITE RICE

2 CUPS CHICKEN STOCK

2 TSP. SALT

1 TSP. DRIED THYME

$^1/_2$ TSP. DRIED MARJORAM

1. Heat oil in a medium frying pan. Add onion and cook until soft. Add garlic and cook for 30 seconds.

2. Stir in rice, chicken stock, and spices. Bring to a boil, then turn down to simmer.

3. Cover and cook about 30 minutes or until rice is soft. Stir occasionally.

Index

There is no love sincerer than the love of food.

— G. B. Shaw

My tongue is smiling.

~ ABIGAIL TRILLIN